A013456091

 D1810317

WITHDRAWN FOR SALE

How to Design, Build and Maintain Your Swimming Pool

by the same author

Gardens Are for Eating

Gardening with Ease

Gardening in the East

Gardening from the Ground Up

America's Great Private Gardens

The Winter Garden

All Your Home Building and
Remodeling Questions Answered

How to Design, Build and

Maintain Your Swimming Pool

Stanley Schuler

Macmillan Publishing Co., Inc.
New York

Collier Macmillan Publishers
London

002 6074206

CHESHIRE
COUNTY
LIBRARY

5 DEC 1975

690.89

WLN 003416

3J 7W

Copyright © 1974 by Stanley Schuler

All rights reserved. No part of this book may be reproduced or transmitted in any form or by any means, electronic or mechanical, including photocopying, recording or by any information storage and retrieval system, without permission in writing from the Publisher.

Macmillan Publishing Co., Inc.
866 Third Avenue, New York, N.Y. 10022
Collier-Macmillan Canada Ltd., Toronto, Ontario

Library of Congress Catalog Card Number: 73-2744

First Printing 1974

All photographs by the author except as noted. Many of the photos were taken for an earlier book, *America's Great Private Gardens.*

Drawings by Wayne Williams

Printed in the United States of America

Contents

How to Design, Build and Maintain Your Swimming Pool

1 Getting Started on Your Pool-building Project

Several years ago a young man who ran a thriving floor and window cleaning service in my community knocked at my office door and asked if he could come in for a minute and talk about swimming pools.

He had been doing our kitchen floor for about half a year, and during his monthly visits he and I often talked about the various problems of keeping a home in good repair. So he knew that I had written a lot about building and maintaining houses and gardens. And he knew that I owned a swimming pool and had occasionally complained about it. His request, therefore, was no surprise.

"My wife and I got to talking the other night about building a swimming pool," he said. "I'd like to know what you really think about owning one."

"We couldn't be happier," I answered. "I admit that before we bought this house and got a pool along with it, I wasn't much interested in having a pool. I'd gotten the idea, working on a few stories, that an awful lot of pool owners were sort of unhappy. And as you know, we've had our problems, too; but in the final analysis they don't mean much. We love the pool because of its beauty, because it gives us exercise we need, because it's a delight on hot days and humid nights. But mostly we love it because it gives so much pleasure and happiness to our children and grandchildren—and to us—when they visit. It's kind of the cement that binds us all together."

"Well, it just seems to us we need a pool for our kids, too. And we'd also enjoy it," the young man said, and went on to spell out his reasons which were, without exception, flawless. And then he turned to more basic matters: "But what I really want to know— if we should build a pool—is what kind? And who builds it? And what about cost?"

"Now you're asking questions you should answer—not I," I said. "Let me loan you a couple of booklets I've picked up. But what you really should do is go down to West Haven with your wife and spend some time talking with the pool dealers on the Post Road. See what they have to offer. And then you ought to talk with some other people around here who own pools. Building a pool is something to take time over. Next to your house, it's probably the biggest purchase you'll ever make."

But my advice evidently didn't sink in. It was only a couple of weeks later that I heard indirectly that our one and only local pool builder was about to put in a pool for the young man.

For the sake of proving a point, it would be nice to say his experience was disastrous. But I can't. He never came back to work on our floors (perhaps because he needed more lucrative commercial work to pay for the pool). We never, in fact, set eyes on him again. So I have no idea whether his pool has been a failure or a success.

I hope it's the latter, of course. But if it is, the man was lucky.

I don't mean by this that building a swimming pool is necessarily fraught with peril. And I don't mean that running a swimming pool is necessarily a burden. If either of these things were true, there wouldn't be approximately one million residential swimming pools in the United States today. Americans may be impulsive pleasure-seekers, but they don't make a habit of asking for trouble.

What I do mean is that the building and owning of a swimming pool constitute an undertaking of sufficient magnitude and complexity to make the outcome uncertain. Hence it makes great good sense to enter into the undertaking slowly and with your eyes wide open.

The best thing you can do is to ask questions—many questions —not just of the people who are involved in the design, construction and landscaping of swimming pools but most especially of the people who already own pools. Pool owners, I find, are remarkably candid about pool ownership. In this respect they differ from owners of, say, boats and expensive automobiles because they don't seem to feel any necessity for justifying their purchases. If you ask them for an opinion about their pools, they give you an answer, good or bad, flat out.

What are the questions you should ask?

They will differ with your reasons for wanting a pool, your financial situation, your feelings about your home, your attitudes toward friends and neighbors, and so forth. But the following questions are basic:

What Are the Dangers of Owning a Swimming Pool?

There are, of course, the obvious ones—the ones you don't want to think about but which you must at least recognize. People drown in pools, they're electrocuted, they have concussions, they break their arms, they skin their knees, they contract diseases. Whether it is full, partially full or empty, a pool is a constant hazard. It can be made safer if you take sensible precautions. But in practice, if not in theory, it can never be totally safe. This is a fact you must live with if you have a pool. If you can't accept it, you'd better not have a pool.

The other dangers of a pool are less serious but more common. They stem from the fact that swimming pools attract people who don't own swimming pools. As a result, unless you take firm steps to control use of your pool by those outside your immediate family, you run the risk, figuratively, of being run right out of the pool or losing friends you'd like to keep.

What Are the Dangers of Building a Swimming Pool?

These are much more easily avoided than the dangers of owning a pool, and yet hundreds of people every year are hurt by them.

The plain fact is that the swimming-pool industry has cheats: Men who advertise a pool at a bargain price and then refuse to sell at that price. Men who offer a special deal on a pool because they "want to use it for advertising purposes" and then renege. Men who purport to represent a reputable company and then peddle the contract to the lowest bidder; who get customers' signatures on "estimates" which turn out to be binding contracts.

And then there are the incompetents and the responsibility-dodgers and the people who promise to come around tomorrow to make repairs and never bother to appear.

Other industries are cursed with the same kinds of slippery and shoddy characters; and there is no evidence that the swimming-pool industry is worse than they. But in a small industry the bad apples stand out.

What Impact Will a Pool Have on the Beauty and Use of Your Property?

Second only to the house, a swimming pool is the dominant feature of the average-size property. It is big. It is highly visible. And it is the focal point for most outdoor activities. For these reasons, its importance should be underplayed so that it doesn't completely overpower the property. But in all too many cases it is allowed to become, in effect, the tail that wags the dog.

How this comes about I am not quite sure but I suspect the fault is attributable equally to the home owner and the pool builder. The former, thrilled with his decision to put in a pool, wants to locate it where it will show off to best advantage to neighbors and visitors. The latter seeks to abet this effort simply because he is

Designed by Lawrence Halprin, famed landscape architect, this pool, despite its carefully sculptured look, achieves great naturalness from the fact that its edges flow in and out around a group of ancient overhanging oaks and a small rock garden just visible in the foreground. Above the garden to the right is a big, octagonal poolhouse. The water from the filter tumbles out of the wooded hillside behind the camera, over rocks, into tiny pools and through crooked sluiceways into the pool.

immersed in swimming pools and their "importance" to the world.

Nothing much can be done about the pool-builder's attitude. It come to him naturally. But while the owner's attitude is also natural, he should do his best to restrain it. Failing to do this, he should seek help from some neutral party who can view the situation dispassionately.

Such a person needs only to combine a sense of practicality with some feeling for design. But if you have a little extra money to play with and long for perfection in your swimming pool, you would do well to call in a landscape architect. More than anyone else, he has the training, skill and sensitivity required to visualize your property as a whole and to fit in your pool so it is but one of the several elements that give the property beauty and make it functionally useful overall.

4

*A boomerang-shaped vinyl-liner pool in an attractive setting. The raised wood deck allows swimmers to get away from the immediate hubbub of poolside activities. The fence with semi-rustic pickets is as effective as a chain-link fence in keeping out intruders and far prettier. It makes an excellent background for shrubs and trees. (*PHOTO BY M. J. MEYERS FOR PRINCE HILL POOLS*)*

How Can You Maximize Your Pleasure in Your Pool?

Most of the answers are to be found in the following chapters. I have just two additional points to make here:

First, consider employing a landscape architect not just to integrate the pool into the landscape but actually to design it. He is an expert. The majority of the most beautiful swimming pools in the United States were designed by members of his profession.

Second, plan your pool during the summer. Since you will be using it in the summer, you will then be able better to appreciate how it should be designed, situated and equipped. For example, if you picked the location for your pool in the winter, spring or fall, you would have only a vague—and probably an inaccurate—idea of how much the pool would be in the sun and how much it would be in the shade during the summer. But if you pick the location in

5

the summer, you can quickly determine whether the pool would get plenty of sun in the afternoons, when you would most probably be using it. In addition, you can tell whether the glare from the pool would make life unbearable on the deck area designed for just sitting, talking and contemplating the delights of poolside living.

How Will You Finance the Pool? Happily, assuming you are a solid citizen with a good credit rating and reasonable equity in your home, you will have no trouble securing whatever financing you need. If you buy a pool from a large pool dealer or builder, he can probably arrange financing for you through a bank or credit corporation in the same way an automobile dealer arranges financing on a car. The alternative is for you to go directly to a bank and make arrangements for a home-improvement loan at normal home-improvement rates and payable over the normal five to seven years.

These are the usual ways swimming pools are financed. Other possibilities are to take out a personal loan from your bank, borrow against your life insurance, refinance the mortgage on your home or "open-end" your home mortgage.

Or perhaps all you have to do is withdraw the money from your savings account.

2 Types of Swimming Pool

Swimming pools are often categorized according to their shape or to the material of which they are built; but there are actually only two basic types—the in-ground pool and the above-ground pool.

In-ground pools have been built for roughly five thousand years, and they haven't undergone any basic changes in all that time. Thanks to modern filtering systems and chemicals, the water in our pools is undoubtedly clearer and purer. And we construct pools out of more materials. Nevertheless, an in-ground pool built in the Indus River Valley five millenniums ago might well be mistaken for some of the more elaborate in-ground pools we put in today. It is simply a great big tub or vat sunk in the ground.

At least, that is what an in-ground pool is supposed to be—and what it usually is. But every once in a while you run across a pool which is not really in the ground but is called an in-ground pool anyway because it is partially dug into a hillside or because it is surrounded by such a vast deck that it gives little impression of rising above the ground.

If such deviants from the norm raise some doubts about the validity of the in-ground name, don't let them bother you. The first characteristic of an in-ground pool is that it appears to be recessed in the ground whether it actually is or not. The second characteristic is that it is a permanent installation. The third characteristic is that it is fairly large—usually measuring more than 15 by 30 ft. The fourth characteristic is that its cost usually runs into four or more figures.

Despite the money involved, in-ground pools offer several advantages:

(1) They increase property value, as a rule. How much is hard to say. But because of the growing allure of residential pools, it is probable that most homeowners who build a pool retrieve at least the initial cost of the pool when they sell their homes; and they may even make a profit. But remember that this happy situation depends on finding potential buyers who either want or think they want a swimming pool. I know at least two people who would not even consider buying a home with a swimming pool because for one reason or another they find pools anathema.

(2) An in-ground pool contributes to—or at least should contribute to—the beauty of the property. It not only serves as the

focal point in the landscaping scheme, but also enhances the scheme by its lines. The principal contribution of a pool, however, is made by the water in it. Water looks clean and cool. It glistens and dances in sun and breeze. It reflects the sky and the surrounding planting, thus doubling their beauty. Finally, its smooth surface serves as a foil for the strongly textured trees, shrubs and flowers.

But the main point to note is that an in-ground pool does all these things because it is at ground level—where you expect to find water in Nature and where you can see it easily.

(3) While in-ground pools are in one respect dangerous (because they are easy to fall into), they are in another respect safe because a parent watching from the house does not have to be at an elevation to see if anyone has fallen in.

(4) You can design an in-ground pool to any size and shape you like; there is no need to limit your choice to the prefabricated, or packaged, pools which are available.

(5) The water in an in-ground pool can be heated efficiently and at relatively low cost because the soil around it prevents rapid loss of heat through the sides.

(6) An in-ground pool is easy to enclose for winter use.

Above-ground pools were introduced in the mid-1950's. Their purpose was to allow families to swim at home on small lots at minimum cost. This is still their primary value.

Above-ground pools are prefabricated units which can be easily and quickly erected on any flat area; and they can be disassembled just as easily if you move. They are, in short, portable and are often called portable pools rather than above-ground pools. This is their second advantage.

Above-ground pools are reasonably safe because they are usually only 4 ft. deep and because it is necessary for someone to climb up a straight wall before he can fall into them.

Finally, unlike in-ground pools, above-ground pools are usually not taxed.

But this ends the good things to be said for pools of this type.

Although it is possible today to buy much larger above-ground pools in more different shapes than 15 years ago, the choice is still limited.

Many of the pools are cheaply built.

Worst of all, they are hideous; and the only way they can be concealed on a flat lot without detracting from the appearance of the lot is to tuck them off in a corner and completely surround them with high shrubbery, walls or fences. The idea that you can achieve the same effect just by massing shrubs around the base of the pool doesn't work, because what you have then is a saucer of water floating incongruously on a tuft of leaves.

On a hillside sloping away from the house an above-ground pool is less objectionable because it can be dug into the hill, surrounded by a deck and thus made to appear like an in-ground pool from the top of the hill (but not from the bottom). But even in this ideal situation, most above-ground pool owners persist in placing their pools in the most conspicuous part of the yard so that all the world can see that they, too, have money for backyard fun and games.

I have included a very short chapter dealing a little further with above-ground pools at the end of this book; but that is the only additional coverage they get. This book is really concerned with in-ground pools.

3 Pool Sizes and Shapes

The size and shape of the pool you build depends on several things:

(1) How much you are willing to spend. Of course, you can't answer this question until you find out roughly how much you *must* spend. Here are the average 1972 swimming-pool prices reported by *Swimming Pool Weekly/Swimming Pool Age*:

	Average smallest pools (15' × 30' and under)	Average middle range (15' × 30' to 20' × 40')	Average over 20' × 40'
Northwest	$4,025	$5,876	$7,942
California-Hawaii	4,033	5,574	7,565
Southwest	4,278	5,314	6,879
Rocky Mountain	4,954	6,702	11,346
Midwest	3,309	5,279	9,630
Florida	4,392	5,218	7,622
South	4,450	5,429	8,268
Northeast	3,134	4,919	7,475
Average All U.S.	$3,922	$5,278	$7,887

(2) How much space you have for a pool, where it is situated and how it is shaped and contoured. I am sure that anyone who is absolutely determined to have a swimming pool can satisfy his desire no matter how "impossible" his property may be. But if you are to be completely happy with a swimming pool, you must site it so that it does not create problems of any sort (these matters are discussed in the next chapter). You must also integrate it with the surrounding landscape and your house.

(3) What your water supply is like. It's true that few homeowners have any worries on this score. On the other hand, if you depend on a well, you may not have enough water to fill even a small pool unless you can make arrangements to have someone, such as the local fire department, truck it in.

(4) How many people you expect to use the pool at any given time. You must be realistic here. That is especially true if you have

children, because they are almost certainly going to bring their friends home to enjoy the pool, too. Overcrowding a pool is not only no fun but also unsafe. The best way to determine how much pool area you need is to use standards comparable to those which have been set by various authorities for public pools. These call for approximately 20 sq. ft. per person, plus 300 sq. ft. per diving board. In other words, if you expect to have no more than a dozen persons swimming at one time, you might plan on building a pool of no less than 540 sq. ft. This would call for a standard 16-by-38-ft. pool.

(5) What kind of swimming you like to do. This primarily affects the shape of the pool, but also affects size. If you or your family are serious swimmers who like to churn up and down getting exercise, developing stamina or training for the Olympics, you should have a rectangular or L-shaped pool—the longer, the better. Other shapes are not conducive to serious swimming. But if you want a pool just to have fun and cool off in, you'll be just as happy with an odd shape.

(6) Whether you want to get your money out of the pool when you sell your house. It is, after all, possible to tailor a pool so specifically to your own requirements that it has little if any appeal to someone else. For instance, I know of a house which has been for sale for some time which has an exercising and racing pool measuring 75 by 45 ft. When you see it, you can't help exclaiming, "What a magnificent pool!" Then you add, "But I sure would hate to have to keep it up."

Pool Dimensions Pool dimensions are extremely variable; but the following are more or less standard widths and lengths for rectangular in-ground pools. As shown, the average depth varies with the contour of the bottoms.

Except for round and octagonal pools, most unusually shaped pools are built to roughly the same dimensions as rectangular pools. In the case of L-shaped, T-shaped and boomerang-shaped pools, the principal arm of the pools is also built to roughly these dimensions.

Regardless of the size of a pool, however, you must remember that considerable additional space is required alongside it so you can walk, sit, dive, vacuum the bottom and so forth. As a rule, such space is provided all the way around the pool; but sometimes —particularly in the case of naturalistic pools—the space is provided only at one side and at one or both ends. Whatever your situation may be, you should figure that this space—whether paved or grassed—should be no less than 3 ft. wide in order to assure safe passage of walkers. Twice as much space is required for sitting by the pool.

Width and length (ft.)	Surface area (sq. ft.)	Average depth (ft.)	Volume (gal.)
12 × 24	288	5	10,800
		5½	11,880
14 × 28	392	5	14,700
		5½	16,170
15 × 30	450	5	16,875
		5½	18,560
		6	20,250
15 × 35	525	5	19,690
		5½	21,660
		6	23,625
16 × 32	512	5	19,200
		5½	21,120
		6	23,040
16 × 34	544	5	20,400
		5½	22,440
		6	24,480
16 × 36	576	5	21,600
		5½	23,760
		6	25,920
16 × 38	608	5	24,300
		5½	26,730
		6	29,160
18 × 38	684	5	25,650
		5½	28,215
		6	30,780
18 × 40	720	5	27,000
		5½	29,700
		6	32,400

Width and length (ft.)	Surface area (sq. ft.)	Average depth (ft.)	Volume (gal.)
20 × 40	800	5	30,000
		5½	33,000
		6	36,000
20 × 42	840	5	31,500
		5½	34,650
		6	37,800
20 × 45	900	5	33,750
		5½	37,125
		6	40,500
20 × 50	1,000	5	37,500
		5½	41,250
		6	45,000
25 × 50	1,250	5	46,875
		5½	51,560
		6	56,250

If you have a diving board at one end of the pool, it will extend back from the pool edge approximately 6 ft. if it is an 8-ft. board; 8 ft., if a 10-ft. board; and 9 or 10 ft. if a 12-ft. board. To these figures you should add a minimum of 2 ft. to walk behind the board.

In other words, if you build an 18-by-38-ft. pool with a 10-ft. diving board, an 8-ft. deck space for sitting along one side, and a 3-ft. deck at the shallow end and along the other side, you must find on your property an area measuring at least 51 ft. long by 29 ft. wide.

But the problems of sizing and designing a swimming pool are not limited to finding space for it on the property. Another job—especially if you put in a small pool—is to determine how much space you need inside a pool for the different members of your family to use it safely and with pleasure. This involves consideration of pool depths.

If your only interest is to swim up and down a pool for exercise, you don't need anything more than a long, almost-flat-bottomed tank with an actual water depth—*not* the depth from the top of the pool coping to the bottom—of 3½–4 ft. (Three and a half feet is the minimum in which a strong adult swimmer can maneuver freely.)

Similarly, if your only interest is competitive diving from a 1-meter board, you don't need anything more than an almost-flat-bottomed, 16-by-32-ft. pool with a water depth of 11–12 ft.

But suppose your family wants a pool in which to swim, dive and just paddle around. Here you start running into difficulties because you need shallow water for children and dunkers and deep water for divers; and somehow you must connect the two areas so a person can walk from one to the other safely.

Long ago, when swimming pools were usually built out of poured, reinforced concrete, the walls were straight up and down from top to bottom, and the floor was flat from side wall to side wall. There is nothing wrong with building pools this way today. As a rule, however, the walls are vertical—or almost vertical—down to a depth of only 3 ft.; and from there they slant or curve in slightly toward the center. In other words, while old pools resembled a tin cake pan in contour; modern pools have a general resemblance to a mixing bowl. Thus you need somewhat less water to fill the pools and somewhat less chemical to treat the water.

Another result of this new shape is that the more or less flat bottom area at the deep end is reduced in size. This does not affect swimming, but it does affect diving because there is less space for divers to plunge to the bottom and come up without scraping on the bottom or side walls. Obviously, this is not a good situation. Consequently, the National Swimming Pool Institute in 1971 introduced a new set of *minimum* standards for residential swimming-pool design. While these standards are actually applicable only to pools built by NSPI members, you should, in the interest of safety, consider them carefully if you design your own pool or work with a builder who is not an Institute member.

The diagrams are necessary to understanding of the standards.

In Diagram A, showing the outline of a pool, Point B is critical. This is the deepest spot in the pool. And for safe diving, the width of the pool at this point must equal a specified minimum. (This does not mean that this is necessarily the widest part of the pool, however.)

The National Swimming Pool Institute segregates pools into five types according to the minimum width at Point B. Types II, III, IV and V are pools large enough to accommodate a diving board. Type I is any pool less than 15 ft. wide at Point B and therefore too small for a diving board.

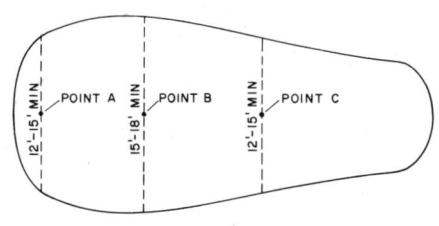

Diagram A

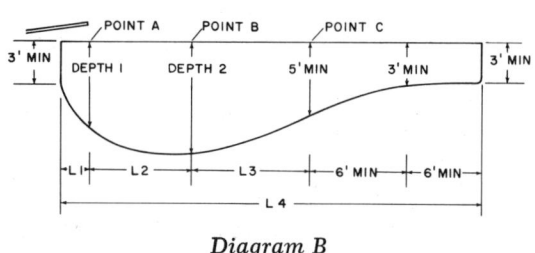

Diagram B

Diagram A (above) and Diagram B help to explain the National Swimming Pool Institute's new minimum standards for residential swimming pools. See text.

Diagram B shows a pool in cross section. At the shallow end, the water depth should be between 3 and 3½ ft.

From the shallow-end wall the floor of the pool slopes gradually downward for a distance of at least 6 ft. The slope should not exceed 1 ft. vertical in 7 ft. horizontal and should be uniform. (A steeper slope is permitted if safety lines are attached to the side walls; but in a family pool, most activity is at the shallow end and such a slope is inadvisable.)

From the end of the gradual slope the floor pitches down more sharply to the very bottom of the pool—Point B. In this area, the slope should not exceed 1 ft. in 3 ft. and should be uniform. At Point C, the water depth must be at least 5 ft. deep and the pool must be at least 12 or 15 ft. wide, according to the pool type.

At Point B an important new dimension enters the pictures. This is the width of the flat bottom area. In actuality, the bottom is not completely flat, because in order to empty the pool, there must be a slight slope toward the drain in the center. But to all intents and purposes, the bottom is flat and the water depth to both sides of the drain (Point B) is equal to that at the drain. This arrangement is essential to protect divers who go off the board at an angle.

From Point B the floor of the pool slopes very gradually upward to a point directly under the end of the diving board—Point A. The deep-end wall rises upward from there. The distance from Point A to the end wall of the pool equals the overhang of the diving board and depends on the length of the board installed.

The chart below gives the *minimum* dimensions for Types II, III, IV and V pools. (Since no diving board is permitted in a Type-I pool, the dimensions of the pool are much less critical.)

Minimum Dimensions for Residential Pools
(NATIONAL SWIMMING POOL INSTITUTE STANDARDS)

Pool type	Depth 1	Depth 2	L1	L2	L3
II	6′0″	7′6″	1′6″	7′0″	7′6″
III	6′10″	8′0″	2′0″	7′6″	9′0″
IV	7′8″	8′6″	2′6″	8′0″	10′6″
V	8′6″	9′0″	3′0″	9′0″	12′0″

Pool Type	L4	Pool width Point A	Pool width Point B	Pool width Point C	Bottom width Point B	Maximum length of diving board
II	28′0″	12′0″	15′0″	12′0″	7′0″	8′0″
III	30′6″	12′0″	15′0″	12′0″	7′0″	10′0″
IV	33′0″	15′0″	18′0″	15′0″	10′0″	12′0″
V	36′0″	15′0″	18′0″	15′0″	10′0″	12′0″

The NSPI Pool Registry Program

This program was established in 1972 in an effort to persuade pool builders throughout the country to construct pools to the NSPI standards and thus to cut down on the rash of diving accidents which had plagued the industry prior to that time. Under the program, if your new pool meets the standards, the builder certifies this fact to the Institute; the Institute registers the pool; and you receive a certificate and plaque (which is supposed to be installed in the pool deck) specifying the type of pool (I, II, III, IV or V) to which yours belongs. The ultimate purpose of this is to prevent a pool builder or dealer at some subsequent date from installing in the pool a new or replacement diving board of improper dimensions.

At this writing, the desirability of the program from the pool-owner's standpoint remains to be determined.

In the first place, there is no doubt that the pool standards themselves are invaluable in promoting safety in residential pools. But it should be noted that the owner of a registered pool has only the pool-builder's word that the standards have been met. The NSPI does not double-check.

In the second place, the registry program was conceived primarily to protect pool builders, not pool owners. In a review and progress report on the program, the October 16, 1972, issue of *Pool News*, "The National Trade Magazine for the Swimming Pool Industry," noted: "PRP (Pool Registry Program) was conceived as a solution to several problems facing the pool industry and NSPI:

First, a growing number of diving-related accidents were happening in swimming pools and pool builders, installers and manufacturers, along with the diving board manufacturers, were being sued for million-dollar sums and huge judgments were being awarded. . . .

PRP, it was hoped, would solve the problem of unfair judgments in lawsuits by giving builders a way of proving their pools have been built according to standards which were deemed safe by the best thinking in the industry. By classifying residential pools into five categories and specifying what kind of diving boards could be safely installed on which class of pools, it was felt that any builder who had built and equipped a pool in compliance with the NSPI standards would find this weighing heavily in his favor in case of a lawsuit.

The diving board manufacturer would have the burden of determining which of his boards would be safe on which category of pools, but once he had so determined and labeled his boards correctly, the onus would be placed on the pool owner if the latter subsequently chose the wrong board in the face of warnings on the carton and on the pool.

Finally, despite efforts of the National Swimming Pool Institute to get all its members behind the program, a good many builders—particularly the large California builders—are ignoring the standards and continuing to construct pools as they have in the past.

If Your Children Are Very Small

Swimming pools designed to the NSPI standards are obviously not suitable for very small children. But you must remember that children do not stay very small very long, and as soon as they reach about six years of age, they don't have any more interest in a very shallow pool than anyone else. So it doesn't make sense to alter the shallow end of the average pool to accommodate them.

On the other hand, if you don't mind spending extra money, there is no reason why they should not have a pool area of their own to paddle in. This can be provided in a separate wading pool which doubles as a garden pool. The alternative is to build a shallow area off the family swimming pool. On a round or kidney-shaped pool, this might be like one of the ears on Mickey Mouse's head. Or if your pool is more or less rectangular, it might be a square alcove off one side of the pool.

The main advantage of connecting a shallow area to the family pool is that the water in it is filtered and treated along with that in the main pool area. A costly separate filtering system is not needed. However, some sort of barrier, such as a fence or life line, is required to keep the children out of the deep water.

Whatever arrangement you arrive at, water depth in a children's pool should not exceed 2 ft. Eighteen inches is a safer figure. Minimum depth should be about 6 in.

Pool Shape

Just what it is that makes so many people today put in swimming pools of unusual shape, I am not sure, but I suspect it is nothing but fadism. The Smiths put in a kidney-shaped pool for one reason or another—perhaps perfectly legitimate. Then the Joneses put in a free-form pool because, well, that's what everybody is doing. Who wants a rectangular pool these days? That's old hat.

This is nonsense.

There's nothing wrong with people building unusual pools be-

This formal, classic Florida pool is overlooked by a vast terrace above a 6-ft. wall (unseen at right). The massive, slidelike piece in the foreground is a piece of modern sculpture. It is made of glistening chrome with brilliant yellow paint on several surfaces.

cause they want to show off, to be different. But to do so just because everyone else is doing it is to display an insecurity for which our forebears would have little patience.

The design of your pool should be dictated strictly by the way you expect to use it, by the setting, by your landscaping plan and by your desire for it to be a thing of beauty and thus a joy forever. If it then turns out to be an unusual shape, that is quite all right. Obviously, that is the way it should be. But to impose an unusual shape arbitrarily on the landscape is to run the risk of tasteless and even hideous artificiality.

My preference in pool shapes is for plain geometric shapes—rectangles with or without slightly rounded corners; circles, and octagons—and true-to-Nature naturalistic designs.

Geometric shapes are good because they are simple; and in simplicity lies beauty. In his essay *Definition of Greatness in Art* John Ruskin, the famous British art critic of the 1800's, wrote:

We are more gratified by the simplest lines or words which can suggest the idea in its own naked beauty, than by the robe and the gem which conceal while they decorate; we are better pleased to feel by their absence how little they could bestow, than by their presence how much they can destroy. There is therefore a distinction to be made between what is ornamental in language and what is expressive. That part of it which is necessary to the embodying and conveying of the thought is worthy of respect and attention as necessary to excellence, though not the test of it. But that part of it which is decorative has little more to do with the intrinsic excellence of the picture than the frame or the varnishing of it.

What Ruskin said about art applies also to swimming pools. A geometric pool has much intrinsic beauty (besides being relatively inexpensive to build and pleasant to swim in). For one thing, the design is clean, honest and forceful. Yet it does not compete for the viewer's attention with the water in the pool—and the water is by far the most beautiful part of any pool.

For another thing, a pool of geometric shape does not complicate the overall landscaping scheme. This is because most lots and houses also have simple geometric shapes; consequently, the pools are readily combined with them to achieve a harmonious effect.

Finally, a geometric pool does not call for a designer of great skill. After all, a rectangle is a rectangle; a circle, a circle; an octagon, an octagon. Once you have decided you should have a simple shape such as this, there is almost nothing you can do to

*A beautiful naturalistic pool.
It is almost completely
ringed with choice shrubs.
The bottom is painted brown.*

*Pool and house are here
integrated physically as well
as visually. It is an interesting way to ensure privacy
and safety in a rather closely
built-up neighborhood. Poolhouse with snack bar is in
the small building at the left
end of the spacious wood
deck.* (PHOTO BY M. J.
MEYERS FOR PRINCE HILL
POOLS)

mess it up. But with a more complex design, if you don't get every line exactly right, the entire design is flawed.

Naturalistic pools are another matter. In design, they are every bit as simple as geometric pools because Nature itself is simple. In fact, if a naturalistic pool is really well done—and if it isn't really well done, it shouldn't be done at all—it is so much a part of Nature that you can't tell where man's work starts and stops. Therein lies its extraordinary beauty.

But no one can say a naturalistic pool is easy to design. On the contrary, it takes great skill—usually the skill of a topnotch landscape architect. Nor is such a pool easy to fit into the average residential property. Perfect integration is usually achieved only if the property has a great deal of natural charm; and as a rule, it must also be of better-than-average size so that the effect is not negated by the surrounding properties.

Lastly, a naturalistic pool is expensive, for whereas you may save money on a large deck and various pieces of equipment such as diving boards and slides, you will probably spend heavily on planting and landscaping. Furthermore, the shape of the pool is likely to be so intricate that construction takes longer than usual.

My argument with pools shaped in other ways—like kidneys, boomerangs, teardrops, wedges, L's, T's, Y's, Z's or like nothing at all: just a freehand design—is not that they are universally unattractive, because they are not. But they do lack the simplicity of geometric and naturalistic pools—which is a strike against them. And to compound matters, they are very, very often built without any reason whatever.

Yet there are times when it would be utterly wrong to put in anything else.

For example, if you have a pie-shaped lot with the house near the back corner and if the zoning code prohibits pools in the front yard, you might not have any choice but to put in a wedge-shaped pool.

Or if you have a very small lot with a magnificent tree smack in the center, you might have to bend a kidney-shaped or boomerang-shaped pool around the tree in order to get any decent swimming space.

Or if you want a wading area for small children but don't want to build a separate wading pool, it would be the height of logic to build an L-shaped pool with a shallow area in the arm.

But I must repeat: unless there are sound reasons such as these for building a pool of unusual design, stick with a simple design which will serve you better—even though less ostentatiously —over the long pull.

4 Siting the Pool

Even if you have a seemingly perfect place for a pool you should not instantly decide that the pool is going to be located there. Pool siting requires a lot of thought, a lot of weighing-this-against-that.

I doubt that many pool owners can say their pools are situated absolutely perfectly. For instance, I am more than happy with mine. But it doesn't please me at all that, when we have a downpour, the water comes off a driveway turnaround about 15 ft. away in sheets, races over a strip of grass, climbs up the slight slope of the swimming-pool deck and cascades into the pool with a burden of sand, silt, hemlock needles and cones, earthworms, etc. To look at the area on a sunny day, you would think such a thing almost impossible, because the grass should soak up much of the water and the slope of the deck should stop the rest. But no such luck. After a deluge, I have a big pool-cleaning job to do.

Of course, I swear a little when this happens. And I tell myself that if we ever move and build another pool, I'll see that it isn't at the foot of a slope. But I am reasonably certain that, while avoiding the silting problem, I'd come up with some other problem.

There simply are so many requirements which must be met when siting a pool that it is virtually impossible to meet them all. Here are the questions you must answer:

Are There Any Zoning Restrictions or Building-Code Requirements Which Will Affect the Placement of the Pool?

Any swimming-pool builder or dealer should be able to answer this; if he can't, a phone call to City Hall should settle the matter quickly. Some of the roadblocks you may run into include the following:

The pool and poolhouse must be set back a specified distance from the lot lines.

The pool must not be located in the front yard.

The pool must be on the uphill side of septic tanks and fields.

The pool must be surrounded by a 4-ft. fence to keep out children.

Water drained from the pool must not be emptied into the city sewers or storm sewers and must be disposed of on your own property in a way which does not create a nuisance for neighboring properties.

Should the Pool Be Close to the House or at a Distance from It?

On a small lot, you may not have a choice. But in all other cases, this requires much soul-searching.

My guess is that the close-to-the-house pool is more popular mainly because it sounds so nice to be able to "fall out of bed right into the pool on a hot summer morning." Other more practical arguments in favor of such a pool are that you can keep an eye on what is going on around it while you're busy in the house; you don't have to go to the expense of building a poolhouse, because people can dress indoors; and you don't have to spend so much for bringing the piping and wiring to the pool. Finally, a close-to-the-house pool is the focal point of family life during the summer. In this respect, it is like a family room. It brings the family together for all kinds of healthful fun and relaxation.

On the other hand, a lot of water is bound to be tracked into and through the house. The sun glinting off the water into the house increases fading of rugs, draperies, and furniture and may make some rooms unpleasantly glary. Worst of all, the pool dominates the view from the house at all times. Even though it may be attractive, it is unchanging. And unless you live in a warm climate where the pool is perfectly maintained the year round, it looks dreadful in winter.

I feel very strongly about this last point because I am convinced that yards and gardens should be and can be as attractive in winter as in summer. But there is nothing at all attractive about a swimming pool in winter when it is shrouded under plastic or filled with leaves.

A pool distant from the house presents none of these problems and, in fact, actually enhances the view (provided the pool isn't covered in winter). In addition, the noise that often emanates from a pool area does not interfere with or detract from life indoors. There is less running back and forth between pool and house; and simply because of this distance, there is more chance for people coming from the pool to dry off a bit before they enter the house. There is less likelihood that people at a party will fall in. And it need not rule family life.

However, the things which are right about a close-to-the-house pool are wrong about a distant pool. But the worst objection to a pool really far from the house is that it may be used at night by people who should not be on your property. To be sure, if no one knows you have a pool, this is no problem; but don't count too much on being able to hide anything as big as a swimming pool from the world at large.

The vast deck (paved with Kooldeck) around this pool flows uninterrupted under the deep roof overhang, through the sliding glass doors, right into the house. The pool, which takes its shape from the lines of the house, thus becomes a permanent, integral part of the house. (PHOTO BY ARIZONA PHOTOGRAPHIC ASSOCIATES)

Which Area of Your Property is Exposed to Most Hours of Sunlight?

You want sun on the swimming pool to warm the water as well as the bathers. This means that the ideal location for your pool is on the south side of the house, tall trees or a hill so that it will be warmed by the sun from morning till night. Thus it is not only exposed to the maximum amount of sunlight during the swimming season but also warms up earlier in the spring and cools off later in the fall.

Lacking a southern exposure, your next best bet is to place the pool where it is warmed by the western sun, because most swimming is done in the afternoon and early evening. An eastern exposure is less desirable because it gets only morning sun. And a northern exposure is, by and large, no good at all, although it is amazing how much direct sunlight it receives during the summer if the house or trees on the south side are low. On the other hand, it is slow to warm up in the spring and cools off quickly in the fall.

Note that these recommendations are less applicable to pools in hot climates than in cold. In those regions, too much sun during the summer raises the water temperature objectionably; consequently, it is desirable either to shade the pool or to cool it by the injection of fresh water. On the other hand, the more sun the pool is exposed to in other seasons, the better.

25

This small, kidney-shaped pool is within only a few steps of the living room, dining room and master bedroom of a hillside house overlooking the Connecticut River. As the picture at right shows, the pool is in effect suspended in a buttressed concrete deck. The pump and filter are installed under the deck overhang under the umbrella.

Is the Pool Area Under Consideration Exposed to a Strong Prevailing Breeze?

If so, it should be avoided because the breeze will carry dirt into the pool and make swimmers feel uncomfortable when out of the water. The breeze will also cool the pool water.

Of course, you could erect a windbreak, but this is not always a perfect solution.

Is the Pool Area Closely Ringed with Trees and Shrubs?

They not only may shade the pool too much but also will clutter it with leaves, twigs, flower petals, fruits, bark, bird droppings, etc. My neighbors built their pool in the shade of a handsome oak and were eventually driven so crazy by the falling leaves and acorns that they had to cut it down.

Is the Ground Flat; Does it Slope Away from the Pool on All Sides; or Does it Slope Toward the Pool?

My experience with rainwater draining into the pool is by no means unique. But it's an experience I do not recommend. That's why you should do your best to find a flat spot or slight elevation for your pool. Failing that, you should take steps to provide a catch-basin-and-drainage area between the pool and the slope above.

Is the Ground Unstable or Does it Have a High Water Table?

These may not be questions that you can answer yourself or that anyone can answer without investigation. But they are extremely important if you want to protect your investment in a pool.

Unstable ground is particularly undesirable because the pool may settle deeper and deeper into it; or it may settle on a slant, possibly breaking the pipe lines; or if built on a hillside, it may suddenly slide down the hill.

A high water table causes less trouble—in fact, none at all—if you are careful to keep the pool filled at all times. But if you leave the pool empty or nearly empty for any length of time, it is quite possible that it will be pushed right up out of the ground by the

The area around this large pool is clearly defined by walls and plants but there is no feeling of confinement. The only obstacles to easy movement around the pool are a few pieces of furniture. And there is nothing to keep the sun off the water all day long.

Few things add as much beauty to a formal garden setting as a swimming pool; and few things add as much beauty to a pool as a well-planned garden. This particular scene is further enhanced by the sight and sound of water entering the pool through a pair of gargoyles. (PHOTO BY THE PORTLAND CEMENT ASSOCIATION)

water underneath. This can happen with heavy concrete pools as well as light-weight vinyl-liner pools. (For a solution to the problem, however, see Chapter 8.)

Is the Ground Underlaid with Ledge Rock?

Blasting to remove the rock can add substantially to pool cost.

Is the Area Free of Underground Pipe Lines and Electrical Conduits?

These can be relocated, of course; but that, too, adds unnecessarily to the cost of the pool.

How Accessible Will the Pool Be to the House?

The concern here is not that the pool is so far from the house that you cannot hear the doorbell ring, or get to the telephone before the caller hangs up, or even see the pool. These are difficult problems but all are soluble somehow. But if the pool can be reached only by a dangerous or tortuous route, that is another matter. There simply is too much movement of people between pool and house to tolerate this sort of thing.

If You Someday Decide to Enclose the Pool for Winter Use, Will There Be Space for the Enclosure and How Good Will it Look?

In the ground, a 20-by-40-ft. pool does not seem very big. But a structure large enough to permit relatively comfortable use of the pool in cold weather is something else again. It covers almost 1,000 sq. ft.; rises 6, 8 or even more feet above the ground. It is, in fact, as large as many houses!

Such a structure is not easy to accommodate on the usual suburban lot; and it may be equally difficult on properties of one or more acres simply because it is in the wrong place from a land-scaping standpoint.

5 Double-checking Your Decision

At this point you have probably reached some preliminary decisions about the type of pool you want, how big it should be, the shape, where it should be placed and roughly what it should cost.

But are you certain that the pool you have in mind is the one you should build?

Since a swimming pool represents a major investment, has a profound effect on the appearance and use of a property, and is difficult to eradicate if it turns out badly, you should now do everything you can to make sure these decisions are correct.

Unfortunately, there is no easy, positive test. But there are several simple double-checks which should help either to confirm your thinking or to indicate that further study is in order.

Talk with Everyone You Can Think of Who Owns a Pool

You have undoubtedly talked already to various pool dealers or contractors to find out about costs, see what they have to offer and get their ideas. You have talked also to pool owners mainly to find out how much they use their pools, what problems they have, whether they feel you should also have a pool and what they know about pool builders. But these were mainly exploratory conversations.

Further talks with other owners of pools—preferably pools of different types, sizes and designs—are advisable now to get more precise opinions about the validity of the decision you have reached. For instance:

"Do you think we'll be content with a 16-by-32-ft. pool?"

"Why did you switch from a kidney-shaped to an L-shaped pool, and are you happy you did?"

"What problems do you think we'll have with a pool in the middle of the terrace?"

To repeat what I said in Chapter 1, I have never yet encountered a swimming-pool owner who tried to convince me or anyone else that we, too, should build a pool. On the contrary, I have found pool owners to be very objective and candid about the problems and pleasures of pool-owning. And the advice they give is good as well as honest.

Draw a Plan of Your Property with All Its Principal Features and the Swimming Pool

This is essential to successful building and use of a pool, though many home owners neglect to take the step. Ask them why, and they'll answer: "Well, it was perfectly obvious where the pool should be, so why waste time on a plan?" Or they'll say: "Oh, we walked the pool out on our lot, and that's enough."

But this is sloppy thinking fraught with possible future unhappiness. You wouldn't build a house without a plan. You shouldn't build a swimming pool without a plan either. A plan may not answer all your questions, but at least it will give you a graphic basis for determining whether the pool you are thinking about will actually fit into your property and whether it is properly placed functionally and aesthetically.

The first step in developing such a plan is to draw an accurate-to-the-inch layout showing your boundaries, house and other buildings, terrace, driveway, large trees and other permanent plantings, rock outcroppings, telephone poles, etc. If you have a surveyor's or architect's plan, start with this: it will save a lot of work. Otherwise, buy a 50- or 100-ft. tape and make your own measurements.

Everything on the plan should be drawn to the same scale—usually ⅛th in. to the foot. Most people use graph paper laid out to this scale; but if you prefer—as I do—to work on blank paper with a triangle and ruler, that does just as well. In either case, be accurate. Measure accurately; translate your measurements on to paper accurately.

When penciling in the plan of the house, show the windows and doors facing the pool or which will be used to get to and from the pool. This will help you to determine not only how accessible the pool will be to the house but also what you will see of it from the house and what, if any, glare from the water will enter the house.

When drawing in trees, show the trunks and also the area covered by the crowns. By doing this, you may find that a tree which you thought was well removed from the pool actually overhangs it. Inasmuch as tree roots normally spread at least as far as the branches, drawing in the crowns may also serve to warn you that the vast pool deck you were thinking about must be redesigned if you don't want to deprive the roots of air and moisture and thus kill the trees.

Finally, when drawing in the pool itself, don't neglect to indicate the deck, filter and heater—and, of course, a possible future poolhouse or pool enclosure.

31

When the plan is completed, have everyone in the family—including the children—examine it carefully. Try to visualize yourselves swimming in the pool, sunning and playing alongside, running back and forth to the house. Imagine yourselves looking out at the pool from the house in summer and in winter: how does it look? Put yourselves, figuratively speaking, in the yard—walking around, gardening, playing tag, etc.: does the pool interfere with what you are doing? does it represent a hazard?

Even if your first examination of the plan indicates that it is perfect in every way, put it aside for a day or two; then take a second look at it. It doesn't pay to hurry when you build a swimming pool.

Lay the Pool Out on the Ground So You Can Visualize It Better

Unfortunately, you probably cannot do this if you are building the pool on a hillside or on very uneven, rough ground or in an area which is covered with shrubs (in these cases, drawing a plan is all the more important because it is the only way you can visualize how the pool will look). But if the pool is destined to go into a reasonably flat, open area, laying the pool and pool deck out full size on the ground exactly where it is to be gives you a better idea than anything else about it.

Use garden hoses to outline the pool; white clothesline for the deck. Here, too, accuracy is essential. If the pool is to be 30 ft. long, make sure the outline is 30 ft. long—no more, no less. If the pool walls are to be straight, make sure the hoses are straight: it is amazing how a slightly curved or scalloped line can confuse the picture.

When the outline is finished, walk around it for a while just looking and studying. Is the shape of the pool pleasing? Does it fit into the landscape? Does the pool look and feel hemmed in by shrubs and trees you don't want to remove? Is it overhung by trees? Is the deck wide enough at all points?

If you are not sure about the size or shape of the pool or its location, change the position of the hoses and clothesline. Then change them again and again. (This is essential if you try to design a naturalistic or unusually shaped pool by yourself, because unless you have been trained as a landscape architect or architect or have exceptional design skill, it is almost impossible to sketch on paper an unusual pool which will turn out perfectly.)

Leave the pool laid out on the ground for an entire day so you can study it as the sun shines down from different angles. (True, you are most concerned about the effect of the afternoon sun because you will be doing most swimming at that time; but undoubtedly the pool will also be used during other hours.) Is the pool in shade at any time? Will the glare off the water hit you in the eyes when you are relaxing on the deck? Will it strike divers on the diving board in the eyes?

One thing which is often confusing about this kind of study is that the outline of the pool looks smaller than the pool really is. Just don't let this upset you. You probably have seen actual pools of the size you want, and you considered them large enough for your needs. That being so, the pool you have outlined must be large enough, too.

Another thing which may interfere with your clear visualization of the pool is the fact that the ground inside the hoses looks exactly like that outside. If this proves to be too upsetting to you, cover the area inside the hoses with newspapers. That will clarify your picture of the pool considerably.

This round pool is set in the center of an octagonal terrace of unpolished terrazzo with a parapet-seat wall on seven sides and an open pavilion (see page 128) on the eighth side. It seems strangely formal for this rugged landscape, but the landscape architect who designed it explains: "The plan was suggested by the lay of the land. I dropped the pool below the lawn level because in situations like this there is often an embarrassment between the natural land and what you are doing. Here we were trying to get a break between land and pool. I wanted at all costs to avoid any attempt to collaborate with nature." (PHOTO BY JOHN D. ECCLES)

Have a Landscape Architect Check Your Plans

This is simply repetition of one of the recommendations made in Chapter 1.

Even though you don't employ a landscape architect to design the pool itself, do give thought to having one look over the plans you or a pool builder have drawn up for the pool and its placement. The cost for such a simple service should be small; but the benefits you reap may be substantial.

6 Choosing the Pool Builder

You can have just as much trouble building a swimming pool as you can have building or remodeling a house. While the great majority of pool builders are competent and responsible, some are not. So you should take plenty of time to select a builder; and you should then take more time to draw up a tight contract with him.

Who Builds Swimming Pools If you look in your classified directory under "swimming-pool construction," you will find a sizable list of firms which presumably fit the description. Running down this will disclose that most of them sell prefabricated pools or packaged pool designs which are made by national or regional manufacturers. These are, in other words, swimming-pool dealers; and in many cases, the only pools they install are the name-brands they sell.

In other cases, however, swimming-pool dealers who sell packaged pools and pool designs are also independent contractors who build pools which are custom-designed either by themselves or by homeowners or landscape architects.

Still other swimming-pool builders are contractors (and perhaps designers) only. A few listed in the telephone book under "swimming-pool construction" build nothing but pools. Others—usually listed under "contractors—concrete," "contractors, general" or "contractors, excavating"—build pools as well as many other things.

(There are also pool builders who are not listed in the yellow pages. Most are contractors building custom pools only.)

Despite differences in the way the three basic types of swimming-pool builder operate, none of them is clearly better than the others. In each group there are excellent firms, average firms and firms to be avoided like the plague.

How, then, do you go about selecting a pool builder who will build a sound pool on schedule and within the cost agreed on, and who will stand behind his guarantee?

The first step, obviously, is to find out everything you can about the people building pools in your area. As a rule, you do this first by paying a visit to the builders' showrooms to see what they have to offer and to get a general feel of their businesses. Sometimes, however, the initial contact is made by a salesman who unexpectedly turns up on your front door step and asks if you'd be interested in buying one of the marvelous pools his company builds.

If this happens, don't accept the spiel at face value. Be sure you visit his place of business and look it over before you become any further involved.

Having formed a first impression of your local pool builders, you should start looking into their reputations.

Checking Up on Pool Builders

Three reliable sources of information are available to you:

(1) The local Better Business Bureau. Actually, the Bureau can tell you only if it has received complaints about pool builders. It knows nothing about honest builders who happen to be only semi-competent. But simply by helping you steer clear of the bad apples, it renders an invaluable service.

(2) The landscape architect (if any) who designs your pool. If he has designed many other pools in the area, he can give you excellent recommendations for or against builders he has previously dealt with.

(3) Previous customers of the pool builders. These are your best information sources provided their names are not given to you only by the builders. The reason: No businessman will release the names of customers with whom he has had trouble. To get the names of a cross section of people who have employed a pool builder, pay a visit to your town building department and ask to see the building permits issued by the department in the past year or two. The permits, which are public property, will reveal the names of all homeowners for whom a pool builder has made installations. Then all you have to do is telephone these people and ask them for their candid opinions of the builder. Ideally, you should also arrange to have a firsthand look at some of the pools he has built.

There are, of course, other clues by which pool builders may be judged; but what they reveal should not always be taken at face value.

Bankers, for instance, are poor judges of building ability, although it is my experience that if you ask them whether so-and-so is a good builder, they almost invariably answer "Yes." But if you question them on a subject they know well—"What's this builder's financial standing? Is he fiscally responsible?"—they clam up and look blank.

Just because pool builders advertise that they are members of the National Swimming Pool Institute does not automatically give them a halo. To be sure, the Institute is making efforts to upgrade the industry, and has established standards of conduct for its members. But it is one thing to get a man to agree to do business in a certain way and another thing to make sure that he does. Furthermore, membership in the Institute is no assurance that a pool builder really knows the business or won't go into bankruptcy before he finishes your pool.

One other thing which is supposed to be indicative of the competence and reliability of certain pool builders is that they sell and install packaged pools or pool designs. The theory here is that the manufacturer of pools, like the manufacturer or automobiles or prefabricated houses, doesn't allow just anyone to represent him in the retail marketplace. On the contrary, he selects and trains his dealers with care, exercises more or less constant supervision over their work, and stands behind the pools they install. The implication is, in short, that pool dealers are better builders than pool contractors because the latter operate on their own without training or backing from a manufacturer.

This is a gross exaggeration of the facts.

I do not belittle the efforts which most swimming-pool manufacturers make to have their pools sold and installed locally by experts. But it is absurd to think that you can put complete confidence in any dealer who handles XYZ pools just because the XYZ Company has franchised him. There are many reasons for this, but the best is that pool manufacturers, like other manufacturers, simply do not have as much control over their dealers as they like to think.

It is equally absurd to think that swimming-pool contractors are any less competent, reliable or honest than swimming-pool dealers because they are small, local firms doing business in their own way without supervision or backing. True enough, there are some swimming-pool contractors who shouldn't be allowed within ten miles of your front door. But others have built such reputations that when Mr. Smith announces he is going to put in a pool, his friend Mr. Jones instantly assumes: "You're going to have the Zalinski Brothers do it for you, aren't you?"

Getting Proposals from Builders

Your second step in selecting a pool builder is to ask two or more of those you have received good reports on to submit firm proposals for your project in writing. The proposals should include a description of the pool, its cost and when it will be completed.

Why should you get proposals and why should they be in writing?

Proposals, or bids, are your best assurance that you will not pay more for your pool than you should. This is not to say that if you ask only one builder for a price, you are certain to be cheated. But when two, three or four builders know they are competing against one another, they are under some pressure to sharpen their pencils and give you the best prices they can come up with. And you, in turn, not only have an idea what your project is really worth but also have several figures to choose among.

Asking for the bids in writing does not bind the builders to those figures. The only figures a builder is bound to are those in the contract he and the customer sign. But when a builder is asked to give a bid in writing, there is a little more pressure on him to bid accurately and a little less likelihood that he will deviate widely from the bid if you award him the contract. Furthermore, builders submitting written bids often break them down so you can see how they arrived at the final figure. This is helpful in evaluating bids.

The actual way you should go about asking for bids depends on what kind of pool you build.

If a landscape architect or engineer custom-designs the pool, he should provide you with complete working drawings and written specifications detailing the materials and apparatus that he wants in the pool. When you ask pool contractors to bid on the pool, you must supply each one with a copy of the drawings and specifications and you must see to it that each one has an opportunity to inspect the site selected for the pool. It is only in this way that you can be certain each builder is bidding on the same project and that you accordingly have a valid basis for comparing figures.

On the other hand, if the pool you have in mind is to be designed by a pool contractor or is to be a prefabricated unit, an exact comparison of bids is an obvious impossibility because there will be too much variation between the pools. All you can do in this case is to tell each builder what you want—say, a 20-by-40-ft. rectangular pool or a 16-by-32-ft. kidney-shaped pool—and where you want it put; and ask him to spell out in detail what he is offering, at what price and under what conditions.

The same approach should be taken if you intend to put in a prefabricated pool but have no particular preference for one versus the others: Tell the pool dealers what you want and where you want it; and leave it to them to give you their proposals.

Selecting the Builder   Assuming that the builders from whom you seek proposals are equal in building proficiency and reliability, the cost figures and construction timetables they come up with should serve as the basis for placing your order. But don't make your choice immediately. Go over the proposals carefully to make sure you understand them clearly. This is especially important if the figures quoted vary widely.

Most people are naturally drawn to the lowest bid; but some almost automatically reject the lowest bid on the theory that something must be wrong with it. Neither attitude is very smart. If one bid is much lower than the others, there must be a reason for it; and you should try to find out what this is before accepting or rejecting the bid. It may be that for one reason or another the builder really is able to build your pool at a much lower price than his competitors. Or it may be that he made a mistake in his figuring, which, if it isn't caught, might cause you trouble in the end.

I know of one low-bidding builder who inexplicably neglected to figure into his bid the cost of removing ledge rock which the owner had told him underlay the area in which the pool was to be located. It wasn't until after a contract had been signed and he started work that he discovered his mistake. When he appealed to the owner for relief, he was told a contract is a contract—sorry. The builder's silent response was to start failing to show up for work every day; and what should have been a two-week, spring building project eventually was completed in the middle of August.

(What the pool builder didn't know was that, if he had taken the matter to court, he might have collected from the owner on the grounds either that he had made an honest mistake in his bid or that the owner knew of the mistake but did not call it to his attention.)

Signing a Contract   Unless you enjoy living dangerously, there must be a contract between you and the pool builder. Whether this is a standard contract supplied by the builder or a contract drawn up by your lawyer makes no difference. But it must be a tight document and you should not sign it until you have read it through and made certain that you understand and agree with everything in it.

The contract should cover all the following points:

(1) The pool should be described in sufficient detail so there is no question about what is supposed to be built. If you have plans and specifications drawn for a pool, these should in effect be made part of the contract although it is not actually necessary to staple them into the contract. The contract simply states that the pool to

be built is that shown in plans and specifications entitled "Swimming Pool for Mr. John J. Smith."

Similarly, if you are buying a pool which is fully described in the pool-builder's literature, reference is made to this in the contract. But if a pool is not described elsewhere, a complete description (size, shape, color, materials, equipment, etc.) should be included in the contract.

(2) The work to be done by the pool builder should also be described. For instance, he not only is to build the pool according to plans but also to supply and pay for all materials, labor, tools, power, etc., necessary to the project. He should also secure and pay for the building permit. And he must, of course, put the equipment in operation after the pool is filled.

(3) How much you are to pay. Usually the sum agreed to covers all costs of excavating and building the pool and installing specified equipment and accessories. But if the builder thinks there is any possibility that he may have to blast or move underground pipes or conduits, he will insist that the unpredictable costs incurred be added to the quoted price; and in that event the contract should spell out whether you are to be billed at actual cost or at cost plus a percentage.

(4) When payment is to be made. Normally the builder receives the entire payment within a specified number of days after you have made final inspection of the pool and given it your approval. If your building code requires that pools be approved by a town inspector, payment is made after that date.

In the case of a large, expensive pool, however, payment may be broken into parts which you dole out as the pool reaches certain points in construction.

(5) The date work will start and be completed. However, the contract should state that the completion date may be extended if the builder is delayed by storms, strikes or other events beyond his control.

(6) The builder will comply with all laws, ordinances and regulations applicable to the project.

(7) The builder will be responsible for damage he does to your and your neighbors' properties, and he will carry liability insurance to cover this. But he is not responsible for removal of trees, etc., which interfere with the project.

(8) The builder will be responsible for damage claims by his employees and is covered by workmen's compensation insurance.

He will also be responsible for injuries to or the death of any other person resulting from his work.

(9) The builder will indemnify you against all liens by sub-contractors and suppliers.

(10) The builder will keep your property cleaned up during the project.

(11) You will carry fire and extended-coverage insurance on the pool and on supplies and equipment stored near it during construction.

(12) The builder will use only new materials and equipment, and guarantees the pool and its important parts, such as the filter, for stipulated periods. The guarantees should be clearly stated so that there can be no misunderstanding about their extent or about who will make good on them.

(13) In the event the builder fails to perform his work with reasonable promptness and diligence or if he goes bankrupt, you have the right to terminate the contract within a stipulated period (say, twenty days) after you have given written notice.

(14) If the pool is to be financed through the builder, the details should be spelled out in the contract.

7 Pool Construction—Part 1

This book is not meant to help families build their own swimming pool with their own hands and weary back muscles, so it does not include detailed building directions. Nevertheless, it is necessary for anyone thinking about putting in a pool to understand enough about pool construction so he can better decide which pool is the right one for him.

The picture has changed considerably since my parents built a pool in the late twenties. In those days, concrete was the stuff of which all pools were made.

Actually, I don't think my parents wanted a pool at the outset—just a pond which could be used as a swimming hole. But the muskrats had such a field day digging through the earthen dam at the end of the pond that was dug that it was soon decided to build a masonry wall across the end and around one side. To maintain a more or less natural look, my parents decreed the wall should be built of fieldstone and concrete, and plastered on the inside with just enough cement mortar to stop leaks but reveal the texture of the stones. But this didn't turn out very well either. For one thing, now that we had a pretty wall on one side, the muddy bank on the other side and the muddy bottom looked pretty silly. For another thing, despite much reinforcing of the plaster coat, the wall leaked a little. So finally a wall was built the rest of the way around the pool and a floor was laid. They were made of poured, reinforced concrete, and they were as tight as a drum. No one noticed that they lacked the texture of the original wall.

That pool is still going strong today: a pretty good tribute to concrete as a building material.

Gunite More swimming pools today are made with gunite (sometimes called shotcrete) than any other material. There are several reasons. The pools can be made in any shape imaginable. They are very strong and durable. There are no seams or joints which may leak. And construction proceeds rapidly (it takes only half a day to gunite an entire pool and finish it for plastering).

Gunite is a concrete mixture which is applied under pneumatic pressure through a hose. First a hole is dug to the exact shape of the pool. Then a grid of steel reinforcing rods and wires is constructed parallel with the earthen walls and floor and about 2 in. out from them. Then the concrete is blown into place behind and over the steel until it is at least 4 in. thick on the walls and 5 in. thick on the floor.

The gunite holds in place even on vertical surfaces because it contains just enough water to make it set but not enough to make it sag. An additive hastens setting. After it is applied, it is troweled and allowed to cure for a few days before it is finished. The smoothness of the concrete varies with the skill of the applicators and the desires and habits of the builder. Because gunite is a dry mortar, it is difficult to trowel as smooth as the average sidewalk; so it is common practice to leave it too rough for painting but just right for plastering. In other words, a high percentage of gunite pools have a plaster finish. But you can have a pool painted if you insist that the builder smooth the concrete adequately.

Gunite application requires not only a good team of workers but also a large rig for mixing and delivering the concrete to the gun. Because it costs just as much to bring this rig out on a small job as on a big job, large pools may be proportionally more economical to build than small pools.

Dry-Packed Concrete   Dry-packed, or hand-packed, concrete pools are made by shoveling a rather dry concrete mix into place on the bottom and against the sides of an excavation which is lined with steel rods and wires as in a gunite pool. The concrete, which ranges from 6–8 in. thick, is then troweled and cured.

Pools made by this method can be shaped any way you like but the walls are given a slight slope from top to bottom to keep the concrete from sagging. (If you want the upper part of the walls to be vertical, it must be poured in forms.) There are no seams or joints. Strength and durability are excellent.

Dry-packed concrete is somewhat easier to trowel than gunite but it still makes for hard work. Nevertheless, most dry-packed pools are given a smooth enough finish so they can be painted after the applicators go over the surface to take down rough spots and fill holes.

Poured Concrete   Poured concrete pools are most commonly geometrical because the concrete for the walls is placed in solidly braced plywood forms and it is not practical to build these in intricate shapes. The forms are usually reusable, thus reducing the cost of the pools and minimizing chances for sloppy workmanship. However, when the forms are removed after the concrete has hardened, it is necessary to obliterate imperfections left by the forms and to trim back and cover the heavy wires used to keep the forms from spreading apart under the weight of the concrete.

Because of the reinforcing steel in the walls and floor, poured concrete pools are equal to gunite and dry-packed pools in durability and resistance to cracking. In the past, however, leaks sometimes occurred between the walls and floor because they were constructed separately, as in the basement of a house. (The walls were vertical to the full depth of the pool and rested either on wide footings or on the floor.) Today, this is less of a problem because the walls and floor are poured together to form a monolith. This is made possible by using wall forms which are less than 5 ft. high and which are open at the bottom. As the concrete is packed down into the forms, some of it oozes out the bottom and is spread out over the floor, which slopes down toward the deep diving area and the drain.

Concrete Blocks If you insist on building your own pool, you will find it easier to work with concrete blocks than with poured or dry-packed concrete. Even so, it's a big job.

The blocks are used only in the walls, which rest on wide footings of poured concrete. If interlocking blocks are used, they are laid up dry. Conventional blocks are laid in mortar as in a basement. In either case, as the walls are erected, vertical and horizontal steel reinforcing rods are woven into them; and the openings in the blocks are finally filled with concrete grout to tie them all together permanently. The completed walls are then plastered.

The floor is made of poured, reinforced concrete 4–6 in. thick.

No matter how carefully a concrete block pool is constructed, it is less strong than other concrete pools and more likely to leak. Furthermore, although it is possible to build a wall with a gentle curve, most walls are straight.

Fiberglass-Concrete This is not a mixture of materials but a combination; and it appears to be gaining in popularity. Vertical fiberglass panels 3 ft. high are used to form the sides of the pool; dry-packed, reinforced concrete forms the bottom. The main claim made for the pools is that the sides have considerable "give"; consequently, they resist frost

The following ten-picture sequence shows how a fiberglass-concrete pool is built. The process combines many of the steps taken in building other types of concrete pool and also vinyl-liner pools. First a hole is dug with a back-hoe and/or front-end loader; then it is given its final shape by hand. The contractor here was the Chapman Construction Co.

After the main drain (center of the deep hole) is installed, the bottom of the entire hole is lined with steel mesh and reinforcing rods raised several inches off the ground. Then the big fiberglass panels that will form the walls are set in.

The wall panels are leveled one by one; and after each joint is buttered with tough rubber sealant, it is bolted together. Reinforcing rods are driven down through channels on the backs of the panels into the ground; and the panels are held in vertical position by horizontal rods driven into the surrounding ground.

The plastic skimmer is bolted to one of the side-wall panels and then connected by plastic tubing to the pump. All below-ground joints in the pipe lines are secured with two steel clamps, rather than the usual one. When the pool deck is poured, the skimmer will be completely enclosed in concrete.

The fiberglass walls are completed and the coping, which is made in long lengths that slip over the tops of the wall panels, is in place. Note that the shallow-end steps are formed into one of the wall panels.

The floor of the pool is formed with dry-packed concrete. The concrete is placed under and behind the fiberglass walls and built up for several inches on the walls so they are firmly anchored. The cratelike device the young workman is using is a tamper.

Forming the entire bottom of this 16-by-36-ft. pool took five experienced young men one day of grueling labor. A cement truck mixes the very dry concrete and chutes it into the pool as it is needed. Three men then place and pack the concrete on the walls and floor shovelful by shovelful. At the same time, two other men tamp and trowel the concrete smooth.

Following completion of the bottom, the excavation behind the walls is filled with crushed stone and a concrete deck is poured on top of this. In this installation, the finished concrete forms only a narrow strip of pavement because the main part of the deck was paved by another contractor with rectangular flagstones.

The U-shaped stands for the diving board are embedded in concrete. The fiberglass-covered board is then bolted to the rear stand. It simply rests on a rubber cushion encasing the forward stand.

Before applying two coats of concrete paint, a workman goes over the floors with a smoothing tool to take down rough spots. Holes are filled with quick-setting cement. Note the ledge at the top of the floor. It extends entirely around the deep end of the pool.

damage better than all-concrete pools. In addition, the coping is simply slipped over the sides so that it can move up and down with changes in earth pressure.

The fiberglass panels are joined together with bolts and tough caulking compound; and as they are erected, they are reinforced with steel rods and anchored into the ground behind them with more rods. When the floor is built, an 8-in. thickness of concrete is packed behind, under and in front of the panels so that they are securely anchored in it. At the deep end of the pool and extending around the sides, the floor is topped by a flat 6-to-8-in.-wide ledge. This permits you to walk all the way around the pool on the inside and thus makes for easier cleaning of walls and coping. Under some circumstances, it might also be a safety feature.

Fiberglass-concrete pools cost more than all-concrete pools; but finishing and refinishing costs are less, because you have only the floor to worry about. The fiberglass walls are integrally colored and so smooth that algae have difficulty sticking to them. But whereas the pools are available in a good assortment of shapes and sizes, they do not offer the unlimited freedom of choice possible with gunite or dry-packed pools.

Stainless Steel–Concrete Pools made of this combination of materials are identical in construction to fiberglass-concrete pools; and in appearance the only difference between them is that the stainless-steel walls are steelly gray on dark days. On clear days, however, they look blue.

The principal advantage of steel over fiberglass is its greater strength; so pools built with it are particularly suited to very cold climates. A less-important advantage is that the steel is even more resistant to algae. The cost, however, is greater. For example, a rectangular 20-by-40-ft. fiberglass-concrete pool costs $7,400, whereas a similar stainless steel–concrete pool comes to $8,000.

Fiberglass-Epoxy Pools made with this new combination of materials might be called a cross between a fiberglass-concrete pool and a vinyl-liner pool, because they have characteristics of both. The fiberglass walls are identical in every way with those previously described. Once they are in place, the earth in the bottom of the excavation is carefully graded and covered with damp sand, as in a vinyl-liner pool. Then the sand is covered with a fiberglass fabric, and several coats of flexible, colored epoxy are rolled into this and up onto the bottom portion of the walls. Thus the bottom and walls are tightly bonded together.

The visible difference between this construction and a vinyl-liner pool is that the bottom liner does not cover the walls all the way up to the coping. The invisible difference—until you examine a sample—is that the bottom liner is almost ¼ in. thick and is much less flexible than vinyl. Consequently, it stays in place better; is more resistant to damage. For this you pay about $100 extra. On the other hand, because of the newness of the material, its life expectancy is not well established.

Vinyl Liners Vinyl-liner pools are constructed by digging a large hole and building rigid, vertical, 3-ft. walls around the sides just below ground level. These may be made of poured concrete or concrete block, but are usually made of prefabricated steel, aluminum, fiberglass or wood panels which are bolted together and braced from behind so they will resist the pressures of earth and water. The steel is usually galvanized to resist corrosion; wood is impregnated with a preservative.

When the walls are completed, the excavation is brought to final shape. Then fine sand is poured in and raked, dampened and tamped to form the sub-floor of the pool. This is usually made 1–2 in. thick to provide a solid, smooth cushion for the vinyl. But some builders prefer to cover the ground with a 2–4-in. thickness of light-weight concrete in order to assure that stones cannot puncture the vinyl and that the vinyl will not wrinkle or sag (as it does sometimes when a sand base shifts or settles).

As soon as the sub-floor is leveled, the heavy vinyl liner, which has been prefabricated in the pool manufacturer's plant, is lowered into the pool by a team of workers, poistioned and attached just below the coping. (Clamps rather than permanent fasteners are used to attach the liner so that it can be easily replaced at a later date.) Then the liner is smoothed out with long-handled brushes and a vacuum-cleaner hose is inserted underneath to remove air bubbles. Finally the pool is filled with water to stretch the liner into all corners and eliminate any wrinkles missed by the workmen.

Although the idea of a pool lined entirely with a flexible fabric may seem far-fetched, vinyl-liner pools have been proved by twenty years of usage and today run a close second in popularity to those made of gunite. That they are not first may seem surprising in view of their advantages. For one thing, they can be installed and put into service more rapidly than concrete pools, and they may be as much as one-third cheaper. The smooth, one-piece, integrally colored liners are satin-smooth to the touch, discourage algae concentrations and are easily cleaned. Since the liners never need to be refinished, the pools never need to be emptied and refilled; consequently, they are ideal in water-short areas and on country properties with inadequate wells. Finally, this is the best type of pool for do-it-yourself construction. Several manufacturers, in fact, offer detailed instructions for amateur builders.

However, in the minds of many people there is an impermanence about vinyl-liner pools. Although the liners carry a guarantee of up to ten years, they eventually deteriorate and need to be

It takes several men to position a vinyl liner in a pool, especially when the pool is an irregular shape. When the liner is finally in place and clipped under the coping, the workmen smooth it against the sides and bottom with brooms, and pull out air bubbles with a vacuum cleaner. (**PHOTOS BY FOX POOL CORP.**)

replaced at a cost of several hundred to a thousand dollars. In the past, at least, the rigid side walls have not always proved as indestructible as they should be. The liners can be punctured and torn (although they can also be readily repaired). Finally, the pools cannot be produced in such a myriad of shapes as can gunite and dry-packed pools.

8 Pool Construction—Part 2

If there is any drama in pool-building, it is to be found in the construction of the shell which holds the water. But this actually is just one phase of the job. Pool-building involves a number of steps.

When to Build
In theory at least you can build a swimming pool any time when the ground is free of frost and diggable and the temperature is high enough to permit concrete to set and cure properly. (Even though there may not be a speck of concrete in the pool itself, it is more than likely that concrete will be used around the pool.)

This means that if you live in a warm climate you can put in a pool at any time of the year. In colder areas, however, most people undertake the project in the spring or summer in the hopes of enjoying the pool that year. But autumn is also a popular building period because pool builders sometimes lower their prices at that time and because you can be sure of getting maximum use out of the pool the next year.

Regardless of when you build, the weather has final control over the pool builder. He can't or won't work when it rains. That is pretty obvious. But what is not so obvious is that he may not be able to work in good weather if earlier you had heavy rains or snow which raised the water table to within about 8 ft. or less of the ground surface. The actual effect this high water has depends on the builder and the particular situation. From experience, he should know whether he can keep an excavation pumped out until the pool is in and ready to be filled, or whether he must delay construction until the water table subsides.

Digging the Hole
One of the stories told about the actor from whom I bought my home and swimming pool is of the time he built the pool. He and my peppery neighbor to the east detested each other thoroughly. So when the pool builder pointed out that he was going to have trouble getting a front-end loader and trucks into the site of the pool, the actor instructed him to knock down the neighbor's stone wall and come in over his field. Happily, the neighbor was out of town at the time and didn't discover what had happened until after the pool was finished.

Few if any homeowners would dare to emulate the actor's

example; but more than one person has had to ask a neighbor—ever so diplomatically—if it would be permissible for a pool builder to come in over his land. This is because the wheeled equipment required in pool-building is large; and sometimes homeowners just do not have any way to get it across their own properties to the pool site.

Here, in short, is one of the first things you should worry about when you consider putting in a pool. Is there ready access to your pool site for a front-end loader and/or backhoe and the trucks needed to carry away the soil? Is there room for the loader or hoe to maneuver?

Soil Problems   Actually, these are problems a good builder should know how to cope with—and should cope with—without any intervention on your part. But be prepared, just in case.

If for some reason you must build your pool on filled ground or in an area with unstable soil (see Chapter 4), it is essential that foundations for the pool be established on firm ground beneath the fill. The least expensive way to do this is to dig down to the firm ground and build concrete piers to support the pool. The piers should be spaced about 3 ft. apart under the entire bottom of the pool and around the perimeter.

Heavy soil—especially clay—poses another problem. When it becomes filled with water, it expands and pushes against the sides of a pool; and if the water freezes, it exerts even greater pressure. To counteract this, you should make sure that, when the excavation around the pool is backfilled, the builder uses gravel or crushed rock, not the soil he dug out.

Water Supply   Although the water in a pool is chlorinated and filtered to make it clean and safe even to drink, state and city health departments stipulate that the water with which the pool is filled initially and which may be added later must also be potable. So if you fill your pool from a well or have water brought in by a tank truck, you should make sure it is pure.

The easiest way to fill a pool is simply to run a hose from a nearby faucet; but if you do this, you must never let the hose nozzle become submerged in the pool. Similarly, if you pipe water directly to the pool, the faucet must be installed several inches above the pool deck. The reason for these precautions is to prevent a phenomenon called back siphonage. This may occur when the water pressure in the supply line drops at the same time that the hose end or faucet is submerged in the pool. The drop in pressure creates a vacuum which causes the water in the pool to flow back into the house supply and possibly contaminate it.

The best place to install a permanent supply line is centered under a diving board. The faucet must be placed far enough below the board so it will not impede use of the board or be damaged by it.

A new idea for automatically maintaining the water level in a pool (but not for filling it originally) is a skimmer into which is built a ½-in. water-supply inlet. As the water level in the pool drops because of evaporation or backwashing, the weir controlling the flow of water from the pool into the skimmer presses down on a treadlelike control. This opens the inlet pipe and fills the pool to proper level.

(When rain overfills a pool, you empty it down to the proper level simply by opening the drain line at the filter.)

Plumbing The water recirculating and filtering system is the heart of the modern swimming pool. It keeps the water clean, clear and delightful (but does not keep it pure). And because of it, you can use the same water year after year.

With some important exceptions, which are noted further on, the plumbing system for the average in-ground pool is put together and operated in the following way:

The size of the system depends on how frequently the pool water must be completely filtered. This is dictated by the local or state health department. In residential pools the normal turnover required is once every 12 hours; but if you expect your pool to be given heavy use by many people, the turnover rate might be increased to once every 8 hours.

Water is pumped from the pool to the filter through a main drain at the deepest point in the pool and a skimmer outlet at the water line. A vacuum outlet is also provided for cleaning the pool but is used only during that operation. After passing through the filter, the water is returned to the pool via one or two inlets installed 6 in. or more below the water surface. (In some pools, however—for decorative effect and a bit of drama—the water returns to the pool via gargoyles or in an above-ground channel built to resemble a mountain stream, waterfall or man-made cascade.)

The main drain is a metal or plastic sump about the size of a

2-qt. kettle with a grated top to keep out leaves, stones, etc. The sump usually used in pools with rigid bottoms has a drain hole in the side which is connected to the pipe leading to the pump and filter, and in the bottom is a second opening containing a hydrostatic relief valve. The purpose of the relief valve is to prevent the pools from being pushed up out of the ground by the water pressure in the ground when the pools are empty. The valve opens automatically and lets in water from below the pool when the pressure is great. But when the pool contains enough water to weight it down, the valve remains tightly closed.

(The alternative to installing a relief valve in the main drain is to build it directly into the bottom of the pool near the drain.)

The skimmer removes surface dirt and debris from the surface of the pool. In this respect it is similar to the overflow gutter in a public pool; but unlike the gutter, it does not reduce surface turbulence. The skimmer is a sump built into the side of the pool just below the coping. It pulls in water through a rectangular mouth in the side, skims it over a floating weir, passes it through a lift-out strainer and directs it on to the filter. To keep air from entering the suction line and interfering with the operation of the pump, the mouth of the skimmer is set several inches below the level of the pool water. Pools with up to 800 sq. ft. of surface area require one skimmer, which is best installed facing the prevailing wind. For each additional 800 sq. ft. or fraction thereof another skimmer should be provided.

The vacuum outlet in some cases is built into the skimmer and in other cases is a separate opening in the side of the pool about a foot below the water level. When you vacuum the bottom of the pool, you simply connect a flexible plastic hose to the outlet; open the valve controlling the suction line, and close the valves on the main drain and skimmer lines.

The inlets on the return lines from the filter are placed in the pool—usually at the shallow end—so that the inrushing water will cause a slight current toward the skimmer. For example, if the skimmer is in one of the end walls, the inlets are installed in the opposite end wall. Only one inlet is needed in a pool with less than 600 sq. ft. of surface area or 15,000-gal. capacity; but most residential pools have two inlets. The openings are covered either with an adjustable metal plate to diffuse the water as it enters the pool or with an adjustable eyeball-like device which directs the water up, down or to the side in a stream.

The piping from the outlets and inlets to the pump and filter must be made of extremely durable material. Top-grade flexible polyethylene tubing is commonly used because it is strong; does not corrode or become clogged by salts in water; resists attack by acids in the soil; and does not burst if the water inside is frozen. The last is an important point, because unless the piping is installed below the frost line, it should be drained in winter; but this is extremely difficult to do in the case of the line from the main drain.

To maintain a strong flow of water, the piping should be laid out with as few bends and fittings as possible. One-and-a-half-in.-diameter pipe is used except with very large filters or when the filter must be located more than 30 ft. from the pool.

To assure that joints are both water-tight and air-tight, the fittings should be coated with silicone rubber sealant before they are inserted in the pipes; and all below-ground joints should be secured with two stainless-steel clamps.

Since the pool pump has only a single inlet, water in the two or three pipe lines from the pool is mixed together before reaching the inlet and then enters the pump in a single stream. At the mixing point, each of the pipe lines is equipped with a gate valve to control the flow of water. Thus it is possible, simply by adjusting the valves, to pull in water only from the bottom of the pool or only from the skimmer; or to pull in water from both at the same time; or to shut them both off so you can get maximum suction through the vacuum line.

A gate valve is also installed on the return line to control water flow.

The foregoing, as noted earlier, is the usual plumbing set-up in swimming pools. The exceptions are as follows:

(1) Vinyl-liner pools are not equipped with hydrostatic relief valves for the simple reason that, if they were ever empty, a high water table would push up the flexible bottom anyway.

(2) The main drain is sometimes omitted entirely from vinyl-liner pools on the theory that adequate circulation of water is provided through the skimmer line and that regular vacuuming will get rid of the dirt and sediment that collects on the bottom of the pool. Omission of the main drain is also justified by the fact that vinyl-liner pools, unlike others, need not be emptied for painting or scrubbing of the walls and bottom. In fact, they should almost never be emptied because the vinyl might then be displaced by the

pressure of the soil and ground water underneath. (The only way to empty a vinyl-liner pool without a bottom drain is to use a portable pump.)

(3) Instead of having separate pipe lines from the main drain and skimmer to the pump and filter, some prefabricated pools have a single line running from the main drain to the skimmer and then to the pump. When this arrangement is used, there is no need to install gate valves at the pump: a single valve built into the skimmer is used to control the water leaving the pool.

Pump and Filter The pump and filter are separate units which are coupled together to work as a team. For maximum efficiency, they should be installed as close as possible to the pool. As a rule, they are placed on a concrete platform level with the pool deck. This reduces installation time and cost. A more desirable location is in a concrete pit below ground, however. This must be water-tight and large enough for a man to service the system, open and close valves, and so forth—which adds to the cost. But because the pump does not have to lift water from the pool more than a few feet, if at all, a smaller, less expensive pump may be used. There is also little chance that the main drain line will freeze in winter.

Whatever the location of pump and filter, the pump should be self-priming. Thus it is able to start pumping within split seconds after it is turned on; you don't have to prime it by hand. The horsepower of the electric motor driving the pump is based on the size of the filter and the rate at which the pool water is circulated. The normal range is between 1/3 and 1 hp. All pumps of 3/4 hp or less should be served by their own 20-amp., 120-volt circuits. Larger pumps (and sometimes 3/4-hp pumps) operate at 30 amp. and 240 volts.

Immediately after entering the pump, the pool water passes through a strainer which filters out leaves, twigs and other large bits of debris. Like the strainer in the skimmer, this can easily be lifted out for cleaning. From the pump, the water then pours into the filter.

Filters for in-ground swimming pools operate under high pressure which forces the water through the filtering elements and back to the pool. The pressure is indicated on one or two gauges mounted on the filter.

Three types of filter are in use. One is known as the sand filter, because the filtering element usually consists of several hundred

This high-rate sand filter and pump are installed within a few feet of the pool but within a year or two will be completely hidden by the encircling yew hedge. Like a great many modern filters, this one has a reinforced fiberglass tank to make it resistant to corrosion. Stainless steel is used for the same purpose in other filters. A large, clear-plastic lid on the tank lets you see the water coursing through. This installation has a multiplicity of valves because the pool water is heated in a heat exchanger operating off the furnace in the house.

pounds of fine, white sand. In the largest filters, however, the sand may be combined with gravel. And in a few cases, pulverized anthracite coal (anthrafilt) is used instead of sand.

Early sand filters had large-diameter tanks to compensate for their relatively slow rate of flow. (They were, however, known as rapid sand filters.) In the modern high-rate sand filter the water moves at such speed that tank diameter has been cut almost in half. The tank holds a much smaller charge of sand, and requires a pump motor of lower horsepower. But despite this improvement, the operating principle remains unchanged.

As the pool water pours through the filter, the impurities are left behind in the sand until finally they reach such thickness that the water flow is reduced. This is not only indicated on the gauge but also is apparent in the speed of the water entering the pool. To correct the situation, all you have to do is turn the multiport control

60

The gate valve at left controls the flow of water from the main drain of the pool; that at the right, the water from the skimmer-and-vacuum outlet. In normal operation, both valves are open and the water from the bottom and surface of the pool mixes at the T fitting before entering the pump. But by closing either valve, the suction on the other pipe line can be increased.

handle on the filter to "backwash." This reverses the water flow in the tank and dislodges the impurities from the sand. The dirty water, instead of returning to the pool, is exhausted from the tank into a storm sewer or other disposal area. When the water from the tank finally runs clear, the multiport handle is reset for normal operation and water once again flows from the pool through the filter and back into the pool.

The simplicity of operating a sand filter is perhaps the main reason why this system, the first used in residential pools, is still extremely popular. But other reasons are also compelling: If you happen to neglect to backwash when you should, the filter continues to operate, although its efficiency is, of course, reduced. Maintenance is minimal. The original charge of sand can be used for years without attention. And the filtering action is good.

But the sand filter has one major drawback: Although it takes only a few minutes to clean the sand by backwashing, the pump is so powerful that hundreds of gallons of pool water are wasted in the operation. In areas where water is short, this represents a serious loss which may be costly or even temporarily impossible to make up. A more common problem, however, is to find a way to dispose of the water. You have four alternatives:

(1) You can pour it into the town sewers. In approximately 6 per cent of all U.S. communities, however, the sewer system is so overtaxed that this is forbidden or strictly regulated. And some swimming-pool industry authorities predict that this figure will exceed 50 per cent within the next few years.

(2) You can pour it down a dry well you dig on your property. Anyone can do this. But if you lose, say, 500 gal. of water every time you backwash, you must put in a dry well roughly 4 ft. across and 8 ft. deep in porous soil; an even larger well in clay soil.

(3) You can pour it into a large holding tank, such as a septic tank, and then pump it out with a separate pump and use it to irrigate your garden. But unfortunately, if you keep watering plants and grass with chemically treated pool water, you *may* eventually kill them. And if the water is very heavily treated, it may kill everything almost immediately.

(4) You can simply let the water run out on the ground. But in addition to killing the vegetation, this method requires considerable space to dispose of the water unless the soil is exceptionally porous. (For example, if you dumped 500 gal. of water on hard, dry, clay soil, it would create a puddle 1 in. deep and almost 800 sq. ft. in area.) It follows that it is practical to dispose of pool water in this way only if you have a property which is big enough to encompass an area in which the health of the vegetation is of no concern.

The second type of filter used in residential swimming pools is known variously as a diatomaceous earth filter, DE filter or diatomite filter. It looks and operates much like a sand filter but instead of employing sand as the filtering medium, it uses a very fine, powdery substance derived from the skeletons of microscopic creatures called diatoms. This has such excellent filtering action—considerably better than sand—that you need only about a pound per tank. This is spread in a thin layer over what is known as the septum—a large, clothlike membrane or system of clothlike tubes suspended inside the tank.

Like sand, diatomaceous earth traps the impurities in the water

This DE filter employs a regeneration cycle. When filtering action slows, the handle is pumped up and down to shake the dirt and diatomaceous earth off the filtering element, which is in this case made up of a cluster of clothlike tubes (cutaway view). The vertical cylindrical chamber with two triangular wing nuts on the pump (exterior view) contains a strainer basket which removes large debris before it can enter the filter. (PHOTOS BY HAYWARD PERFLEX CO.)

rushing through the filter tank and eventually becomes clogged. Cleaning is done in several ways, according to the design of the system. In some cases, you simply open the tank, lift out the filter element and sluice water over it. In other cases, you backwash as with a sand filter. Following either cleaning operation, new diatomaceous earth is spread on the filter element; and the filter is put back into service.

A newer system of cleaning employs a regeneration cycle. In this case, when the filtering action slows, you stop the filter and pump a handle on the filter up and down several times. In the swimming-pool trade, this is known as "bumping," because it shakes, or bumps, the impurities and diatomaceous earth off the filter element. Then, when the filter is started up again, the diatomaceous earth is redeposited in a clean layer on the filter element and goes to work once more. With this system, you don't have to recoat the filter element by hand after every cleaning. However, the earth is not reusable forever: after a month or two, depending on how the pool is used, you must bump and drain the filter completely, then add new earth.

DE filters have two advantages: First, if properly managed, they clarify pool water better than the best sand filter. Second, regardless of the way they are cleaned, they waste little water. Even those requiring backwashing use less than 100 gal. As a result, disposal of the water is a simple matter; and in water-short areas, there is little worry about replacing the loss.

On the other hand, DE filters are more of a nuisance to operate than sand filters simply because of the necessity for recoating the filter elements with diatomaceous earth. This can be a messy job. And even the best regenerative filters must be operated perfectly if they are to produce crystal-clear water. Some time ago I asked a senior representative of one of the country's biggest swimming-pool equipment distributors what his experience had been with the DE filter, which is generally rated as the best in the industry. He had used this filter for several years in his own pool; prior to that he had used a top-brand sand filter. He replied that he rated the DE "a shade" ahead of the sand filter because of its superior filtering action. But, he said, even though the filter is extremely well designed and easy to run, he had his problems with it. "And we're beginning to get comments from other people who've bought them. The trouble is that if the swimming-pool dealer doesn't tell you *exactly* how much earth to use and how to use it, you don't get the fine results you should."

The third type of filter used in swimming pools is the cartridge filter. In this the incoming water is forced through a cluster of cylindrical cartridges made of fibers and resins. These filter out particles down to 3–5 microns in size—the same size as the particles removed by DE filters.

Mainly because they are fairly new and made by few firms, cartridge filters lag far behind sand and DE filters in popularity. Their filtering action, however, is on a par with that of the DE filters. They take up less space than either DE or sand filters. And they operate for a longer time before needing cleaning.

There is no backwashing. When the cartridges become clogged —on average, about every three to five weeks—you just lift the cluster out of the filter tank and hose it off under pressure. The cartridges are reusable for about a year, and must then be replaced. The cost of the new units runs from approximately $25 to $40 a filter, depending on the capacity.

Time Clocks

If you run your filter system 24 hours a day, day in and day out, you have no need for a time clock to control its operation. But if you run the filter only 8–12 hours daily, a time clock is a convenience you won't regret installing, because it releases you from bondage. You don't have to remember to turn on the system in the morning and turn it off at night. You don't have to go outdoors in bad weather to attend to the system. And when you're away on vacation, you don't have to choose between finding a human substitute to operate the filter and closing down the pool and allowing it to get dirty.

Time clocks cost between $18 and $30, depending on the design. A single clock will control both the filter and a pool heater if the former is run no more than 12 hours a day. But if the filter operation exceeds 12 hours, a separate clock is needed for a heater.

Installation should be made in a dry location on the power line running from the house to the pool equipment. If you decide against a time clock when you build your pool and later change your mind, it is easy to make the addition without costly alterations in the wiring.

Automatic Chlorinators

The automatic chlorinator is another device that takes work out of running a pool because it injects just the right amount of chlorine into the water day after day without any attention from you and because it uses a form of chlorine which leaves no residue in the water. According to one of my friends, the one trouble with it is

65

that it requires so little attention that she often neglected it only to discover that her pool was no longer properly treated. "When I chlorinated the pool myself, it was a routine, daily job I never forgot," she told me. "But when we put in a chlorinator that needed to be refilled only ever so often, it was hard to remember when I should look at it or when I had last filled it. So I've stopped using it."

I have not heard the same complaint from other pool owners.

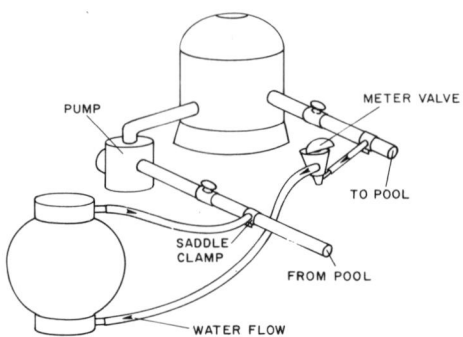

Schematic drawing shows how one type of automatic chlorinator (foreground) is connected to the plumbing system.

The chlorinators made for residential pools are simple devices which cost about $30–$60. Installed close to the filter, they are connected by little plastic tubes to the suction and return lines. The tube from the suction line carries a small amount of water into the chlorinator, where it dissolves the chlorine; then the treated water is returned through the other tube into the return line and thence into the pool. The amount of chlorine entering the pool is controlled by a simple metering valve.

The chlorine used in a chlorinator is a concentrate in tablet or cartridge form. The tablets or cartridges are replaced when they have dissolved. The frequency of replacement depends on the chlorine formula, pool size, water chemistry, etc. It may run from roughly two to four weeks. The cost of the chlorine used in the course of a year is about the same as the cost of hand-fed granular chlorine.

When using a chlorinator, you must begin the swimming season by super-chlorinating the pool by hand (see Chapter 16). After that the chlorinator takes over. By testing the water about every 12 hours for a couple of days, you finally arrive at the proper setting for the metering valve. From then on little adjustment of the chlorinator is necessary except when the weather and/or pool usage change drastically. You must, however, test the water regularly throughout the swimming season.

One of the newest types of chlorinator is a foreign invention now being produced in the United States which makes pure chlorine out of rock salt and automatically feeds it into the pool. Conversion of the salt into chlorine is accomplished by electrolysis in a suitcase-size tank which releases chlorine gas to a separate vessel, where it is mixed with water from the pool. The entire system has an initial cost of almost $300, but the annual operating cost, including the cost of electricity, runs to about only $15. The present system is large enough to take care of any pool of up to about 30,000-gal. capacity. For larger pools, it is necessary to supplement treatment with a dry chemical.

Salt-Water Pools   People who live close to the ocean often fill their pools with salt water, and others with salt-water wells follow suit. And I am sure there is more than one person who does as a friend of mine does: he has a 40,000-gallon, fresh-water pool which he loads with rock salt every spring. The man supplying the salt originally asked Bob what kind of sea water he liked. "I can give you anything from Nantucket to Key West," he said. "I'll settle for Nantucket," Bob answered—which means that he buys 10,000 lbs. of salt a year. If he had chosen Key West water, he would have needed a thousand pounds more.

Salt-water pools present no unusual operational problems, but all the metal parts exposed to the water must be made of stainless steel, bronze or—for a few items—porcelainized steel. The piping is almost always plastic. This requirement adds considerably to the cost of the pump and filtering system, but you would be beset by corrosion problems otherwise. Lesser metals disintegrate in short order.

Coping   The coping is the top of the swimming-pool walls. In some cases, it forms a distinct line which visually separates the water in the pool from the deck. In other cases, it is simply a continuation of the deck.

Normally the coping is not an integral part of the walls and is installed after they have been completed but before they are finished. In some fiberglass-concrete pools, however, the coping and walls are formed out of single sheets of fiberglass. And occasionally in concrete pools the coping is nothing more than the smoothed-off top of the walls.

The standard coping is prefabricated in what is usually referred to as a bullnose design because the front edge, which overhangs the side of the pool, is bulbous. In profile, the top of the coping is shaped like a breaking wave. The idea behind this design is (1) to provide a handhold for swimmers and a comfortable take-off point for divers or people sitting on the edge; and (2) to keep water which splashes out of the pool from running back in.

Bullnose coping for concrete pools is usually made of polished concrete or terrazzo in sections about 1 ft. wide and 2 ft. long. These are attached to the top of the walls with Portland cement. For vinyl-liner pools and fiberglass pools, the coping is usually made in long lengths of aluminum with a baked-enamel finish. It is bolted to the walls or simply clipped over the top. A groove under the nose holds the edges of a vinyl liner securely but permits ready removal of the liner when it wears out.

The cost of both concrete and aluminum coping is in excess of $2 a foot before installation.

A simpler and less costly type of coping made for vinyl-liner pools is a semiflexible strip of vinyl which snaps over the top of the walls and edges of the liner. It is less slippery than aluminum but soils more readily and is harder to clean.

Copings which are an integral part of a deck are made, like the deck, of concrete, brick, flagstone, slate or tile. This does not mean, however, that the paving must be of uniform appearance from the back edge of the deck to the water. Frequently it is. But in many other cases, the paving next to the pool is laid so that it forms a rather distinct strip. For example, in a deck made of bricks laid wide side up, the coping strip may be made of the same bricks laid on edge.

From the appearance standpoint, I prefer an integral coping because I like the sweep of continuous paving. It may also cost a bit less than bullnose coping. On the other hand, it is less comfortable to hang on to when you're in the pool. Because the edge is usually square and sharp, it is much less comfortable to climb up over, sit on or dive off. Finally, if it is made of brick, the edges eventually become chipped.

68

Coloring the Pool

Whoever persuaded the American public that swimming pools should be colored blue did the world a grave disservice. To be sure, blue is better than red, orange, yellow or purple. Even so, when seen from an airplane or when you are walking through the garden, it is a very disturbing color because it is so completely unnatural. Sometimes it is downright garish.

If there is a "best" color for a pool it is white. For one thing, it provides the best visibility whether you're in the water or out. This is the main reason why it is almost always used in public pools. It also provides the best visibility for the least wattage when illuminated at night with underwater lights. In addition, a white pool looks blue during the daytime. True, it is only a pale blue even at the deep end; but it has a much less disturbing, more natural appearance than a pool painted blue.

Green is also an excellent choice, especially for a pool in a sylvan setting, because it links the pool with the surrounding trees and lawn. It also harmonizes with all deck materials, whereas blue does not. My own pool is a pale green which develops a distinct bluish cast on sunny days. The round pool shown on page 33 is a much darker, sharper green, which looks ghastly when the pool is empty but which pales to aquamarine in sunlight.

Grays and tans are occasionally used by landscape architects in naturalistic pools to effect an even closer link with nearby plants and the stones in the deck. As in a river, the water acquires blue or green tints on bright days but is considerably less inviting when the sky is overcast. For this reason, these colors are best used in regions which are predominantly sunny.

Black is the most surprising and dramatic color for a pool. It looks very deep blue in sunlight and has a mirrorlike surface which reflects the surroundings better than any other color. But it greatly reduces underwater visibility and makes a pool appear shallow.

Combinations of color are popular among people who like to paint elaborate designs on the floor and walls of their pools. But the most common combination is a white pool with a band of blue around the walls below the coping. The width of the band varies from 6 in. to as much as 3 ft. in pools with fiberglass walls. Regardless of the width, the effect of the band is to strengthen the pale blue of a white pool without giving the overwhelming hue of a blue pool.

69

Finishing the Pool All pools which are made in whole or in part of concrete should be given a final finish before they are filled with water. The job is of critical importance not only to the beauty of the pool but also to its subsequent maintenance. Four types of finish are currently in use:

(1) Ceramic tile is the classic finish for poured concrete or concrete-block swimming pools but almost never used for complete coverage of floor and walls in residential pools, because it costs between $2.50 and $3.50 a square foot installed. (But it is often used in a narrow band at the water line for decorative effect and for easy removal of the scum left by the water.) In addition, the installation requires considerably more skill than many tile contractors have. On the other hand, once the tile is in, it should last indefinitely with minimum maintenance. It is stainproof; unaffected by sunlight, wear or chemicals. Scale caused by hardness of the water can be scrubbed off easily.

Tiles used in pools are usually unglazed mosaics. Standard-grade tiles are satisfactory for outdoor pools in warm climates and all indoor pools; but frostproof tiles must be installed in outdoor pools in cold climates. Before tiling starts, the pool must be filled with water and tested for leaks.

(2) Cement plaster is usually used to finish gunite pools because the gunite is too rough for painting and has too much contour for tiling. The plaster is made, as a rule, of white Portland cement and marble dust, but sometimes fine white sand is substituted for the marble dust. It is applied in one or two coats with a total thickness of approximately ⅜ in. Two coats are preferable because it is easier to establish a smooth, level surface by applying a ¼-in. brown coat followed by a ⅛-in. final coat. Before application is made, the pool shell is allowed to cure for about a week and is then scrubbed with muriatic acid and rinsed. Both the concrete shell and the brown coat must be scratched thoroughly to ensure adhesion of the following coat.

Since most of the marble dust on the market is white, plaster pools are usually white. The shade of white, however, varies with the source of the marble. Marble dust from Georgia stone, for instance, is almost pure white, whereas that from certain areas in Texas is slightly blue-white.

Black marble dust is used to produce black plaster. Plaster of other colors, such as green or blue, is made with white cement and white sand to which special powdered pigments are added; but the plaster thus produced is rarely as uniform in color as white or black plaster and is more subject to fading.

The cost of plastering a pool runs about 50 cents a square foot. Before hiring a plastering contractor, you should make sure that he has had experience finishing pools, because the work is a great deal more demanding than house-plastering. You should also make sure that if cracks or black "burns" appear in the plaster during application, the contractor will redo the entire job; otherwise the plaster will look patched and water will probably get in behind it.

If plastering is done properly, the finish should last for years. But you must be careful not to wash it with strong acid solutions which would etch the surface or to allow steel objects or leaves to rest on it for long, because they make indelible stains. Covering a plastered pool in the fall and winter is therefore essential. Keeping the pool filled with water in winter is also essential, since unprotected plaster may be damaged by low temperatures. Should the surface be damaged in any way, however, it can be repaired and then painted.

(3) Integrally colored concrete provides a very inexpensive finish but is not often used because the concrete must be floated and troweled smooth within a short time after it is laid. This work is easy—comparatively speaking—only on poured concrete floors; but it is also possible—although not easy—on the walls of dry-packed pools.

Since colored concrete is likely to fade, white is the best choice of color. The concrete must be cleaned only with detergents, never with acids.

(4) Paint is widely used on all concrete pools because application is simple and economical. But all paint finishes must be renewed periodically.

Portland cement paint bonds to concrete only and can therefore be used only on unfinished concrete pools, plastered pools or pools previously finished with cement paint. The paint is subject to fading and powdering; has a fairly rough finish that is not easy to clean; has to be renewed (one coat only) every year or two; and is a poor base for other paints. But it is inexpensive and easy to apply with a brush (unlike other paints which are flowed on, it must be scrubbed into the pores). And because it adheres to damp surfaces, it can be applied to a new pool as soon as the concrete has set for about two days. Filling of the pool with water can start 24 hours later.

Another advantage of cement paint is that some formulations have so much body that they can be used almost like plaster to level and smooth rough concrete. (They do not, however, have enough body to smooth out rough gunite. Neither should they be applied to any very bumpy or holey concrete until the imperfections have been removed.) In the fiberglass-concrete pool pictured on pages 45–52, for instance, the dry-packed concrete bottom had an objectionably rough texture. But the builder corrected this by coating it first with a thick cement paint and then with a thinner cement paint. The two coats were applied on the same day. The final finish had almost no texture.

Vinyl paint is different from cement paint in almost every respect. It is so difficult to apply that the job should be left to experts; consequently, the cost is higher than for any other paint. But once it is on, you should not have to repaint for about five years.

Vinyl paint can be applied to all smooth concrete and plastered pools. The surface must first be etched with muriatic acid; neutralized with trisodium phosphate (which is sold under brand names such as Soilax and Spic 'n Span); rinsed; and allowed to dry completely. Since the paint is very thin, about three coats should be sprayed on for complete coverage (but only one or two coats are needed when repainting). The final finish is tough and smooth; and as in the case of vinyl liners, algae and dirt generally do not stick to it. Cleaning is easy.

Epoxy paint is much like vinyl in that it produces a smooth, durable, long-lasting (five or six years), readily cleanable surface. Manufacturers like to claim the finish is "tilelike," and they are not far from the truth. The paint is used on concrete and plaster; and it is the only paint which can be applied to fiberglass (if for any reason you should want to paint a fiberglass pool).

Use a two-part paint, not one which comes ready to apply. Surface preparation is like that for vinyl paint; but as with cement paint, the surface need not be dry or completely cured when you start painting, and you can fill the pool 48 hours after the paint is dry. Application with brush, roller or spray gun is easy even for amateurs.

The principal drawbacks of epoxy paint are that it requires very careful surface preparation when you repaint; and if you decide to switch to another type of paint, you should usually remove the old finish entirely.

Rubber-base paint is the most widely used paint for concrete and plastered pools because it is extremely easy to apply, inexpensive, forms a smooth, readily cleaned surface and should last about three years before it needs to be renewed.

Unfortunately, many of the rubber-base and latex paints sold for swimming pools are not well formulated and consequently give considerable trouble. The only type you should use is a high-grade chlorinated rubber paint. Two coats are needed on a new pool; one on an old pool.

The paint cannot be applied until the concrete or plaster has been allowed to cure for thirty days (but some paint manufacturers insist that this waiting period can be cut in half). Some time during the curing process, the surface should be acid-etched, neutralized and rinsed. When painting starts, the surface must be dry. The paint itself should then be allowed to dry for a week before the pool is filled.

9 Accessories and Equipment

Like automobiles, swimming pools can be fitted out with optional equipment costing in the hundreds and thousands of dollars. They can also be "stripped." Before you start building a pool, it is well to decide how many of the extras you will need. Some can be added at any time after the pool is completed; but others must be installed during construction.

Steps and Ladders Since every pool must provide easy ingress and egress, steps and ladders can hardly be called optional equipment. But you do have a choice of what to put in.

Concrete and fiberglass-concrete pools usually have steps which are permanently built-in at the shallow end. In width these range from a minimum of 3 ft. to the entire width of the pool. The treads should be no less than 12 in. deep; the risers, 6–12 in. high.

In early vinyl-liner pools, access to the shallow end was by a short ladder costing roughly (today's prices) $75. Current pools, however, often have built-in steps of fiberglass. These cost about $500. Set-in fiberglass steps which are weighted down with bricks or concrete blocks are available but they are such a poor—and expensive—reproduction of the real thing that they should be considered only as a substitute for a shallow-end ladder.

Whether you equip steps in any type of pool with handrails depends on the age and health of those using the pool. They may be essential. On the other hand, you should remember that everything which sticks up above the coping interferes with the covering of a pool and the movement of people around the pool. Many such things cannot be eliminated, whereas rails at steps can be.

National Swimming Pool Institute standards call for a ladder at the end of the pool opposite to the steps if the pool is more than 5 ft. deep at this point or exceeds 40 ft. in length. Pools more than 30 ft. wide should have two ladders at the deep end on opposite sides. In all cases, of course, the ladders must be far enough from the diving board so that divers cannot strike them.

All steps and ladders should have skid-resistant treads. For ease of upkeep, ladders and stair rails are best made of stainless steel, but cheaper galvanized units which you paint are available. Both ladders and rails are set into anchor sockets embedded in the coping or pool decks so they can be removed in winter. The bottom ends of ladders should be equipped with rubber bumpers to keep them from damaging the sides of the pool against which they bear.

If step holes in the wall are substituted for a deep-end ladder in a concrete pool, they should be at least 12 in. wide and 5 in. deep. Slope them slightly toward the pool so dirt will not collect. Mount grab rails on the coping on either side of the steps.

Diving Boards   Under NSPI standards, no diving equipment of any description is permitted in a Type I pool (see Chapter 3). The boards permitted in other types of pool are listed below:

Pool type	Maximum length of board	Maximum height of board above the water	Tip of board from Point A (see Chapter 3)
II	8 ft.	20 in. (½ meter)	Plus or minus 3 in.
III	10	26 (⅔ m.)	"
IV	12	30 (¾ m.)	"
V	12	40 (1 m.)	"

There is no reason, of course, why you shouldn't use a shorter board in a larger pool; and you may install it at a greater height than normally permitted. In the latter case, however, the tip of the board must be extended outward for the distance specified for the larger pool. For example, if you want to install an 8-ft. board in a Type V pool at the 20-in. height normally specified for a board of this length, the tip of the board should be 1½ ft. from the deep-end wall of the pool (this would place it at Point A in a Type II pool). But if you want to install an 8-ft. board in a Type V pool at a height of 40 in., the tip of the board must be 3 ft. from the deep-end wall.

At least 12-ft. headroom above the diving board is required in all enclosed pools.

Boards 14–16 ft. long should be used in residential pools only if the pool depth is increased to 11 or 12 ft. and the dimensions of the diving area are increased substantially. (Follow the standards set by either the Amateur Athletic Union or the National Collegiate Athletic Association.)

Diving boards are made in many grades, but for the home pool relatively inexpensive boards carrying a one-year guarantee are more than adequate. Most have a wood core and are covered with molded, skid-proof fiberglass in white, turquoise or several shades of blue. Aluminum boards are also available. The boards are made in 6-, 8-, 10- and 12-ft. lengths and are 18 in. wide.

The boards in common use are fulcrum-actuated—mounted on two U-shaped, stainless-steel stands which are firmly embedded in a thick concrete base. The rear end of the board is bolted to one stand, which may be called the rear hold-down. The middle of the board rests on the forward stand, or fulcrum, which is covered with a rubber cushion. Unless otherwise specified by the maker of the board, the space between the hold-down and fulcrum should be at least 30 in. for a 6-ft. board; 40 in. for an 8-ft. board; 52 in. for a 10-ft. board; and 62-in. for a 12-ft. board. The maximum height of a board above the water is 30 in.

An alternative and increasingly popular way to mount a diving board is to place it on a massive, streamlined, enamel-finished pedestal which is bolted to the deck. This improves the appearance of the installation but does not affect the use of the board or its action. The pedestals are available in four heights (20, 26, 30 and 40 in.) and in three lengths for boards of different length.

Prices for the least-expensive type of residential diving board mounted on U-shaped stands range from about $75 for an 8-ft. board to $105 for a 12-ft. board. The same boards mounted on modern pedestals cost $175 and $265 respectively. If handrails are installed on a pedestal-mounted board, they add $90 to the cost.

As pointed out in Chapter 3, one problem in putting in a diving board is that it takes up a lot of space at the deep end of the pool. But just because you do not have enough space does not mean you must deprive your family of the fun a board gives. The answer is to install a jump stand.

This is nothing more than a short diving board actuated by strong steel springs to give added lift when you bounce on the end. The stands are usually designed to overhang the edge of a pool 18–24 in.; but with one type, no overhang is possible. This makes it dangerous to use; but so far that has not deterred manufacturers from producing it or pool owners from buying it.

Jump stands are available in 2½-, 3-, 4-, 6- and 8-ft. lengths and range from $60–$150 in price. All should be anchored firmly to the deck.

Slides Considerable deck space is also required for a slide, although if you install a curved slide, the actual depth of the deck (from pool edge to the outer deck edge) need not be great.

A small straight slide about 4½ ft. high (6 ft. to the top of the handrails) requires a deck 6 ft. deep. To this you should add another 2 ft. to get on the ladder. A straight king-size slide 10½ ft. high (12 ft. at the top of the handrails) requires a deck 14½ ft. deep (plus 2 ft. for getting on the ladder).

The space savings made possible by curving the slide are illustrated by a 6-ft.-high slide which requires a deck depth of 7 ft. 4 in. (plus 2 ft.) if it is straight, whereas it needs only 3 ft. (plus 2 ft. to get by the side) if it is curved. It should be noted, however, that since a curved slide is placed parallel with the edge of a pool, it blocks access to the pool for some distance. In fact, a curved 6-ft. slide takes up about 11 ft. of space along the pool edge.

The height of the slide determines, in part, where it should be placed, because you need a certain minimum water depth to prevent injury to sliders. For example, a 4½-ft.-high slide needs a water depth of 1½ ft., whereas a 10½-ft. slide should have a water depth of 5 ft.

In all cases, the lip of the slide should project well beyond the pool edge.

Slides are made with fiberglass chutes and aluminum underpinnings. A small pipe carries water from the house supply or a garden hose to the top of the slide, where it flows out over the slide and down into the pool. The legs can be permanently embedded in the deck; but since this makes it difficult to cover a pool, you may prefer to set them in anchor flanges set into the deck or bolted to the top. The slide can then be removed at any time.

Cost of slides starts at approximately $150 for a small unit and rises to $400.

Hydrotherapy Systems These systems are designed to introduce aerated water into the pool through special jet inlets at a high pressure which agitates the pool water and thus gives a muscle-relaxing massage. Relatively inexpensive portable systems are available for installation in existing pools; and it is possible to add a built-in system by drilling through the pool walls and changing the pool plumbing. But it is easier to install a hydrotherapy system when you are building a new pool;

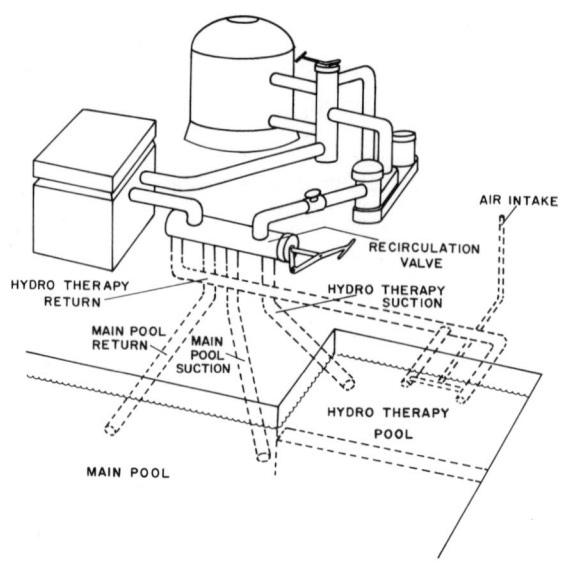

AIR INTAKE

RECIRCULATION VALVE

HYDRO THERAPY RETURN

HYDRO THERAPY SUCTION

MAIN POOL RETURN

MAIN POOL SUCTION

HYDRO THERAPY POOL

MAIN POOL

This illustrates one way to build a therapy pool as an alcove to the main pool.

and although it costs more than a portable system—up to about $500—it looks better.

Installation is made in three ways: directly in the swimming pool; in an alcove off the swimming pool; or in a small pool separate from but usually near the swimming pool.

Hydro systems built into the swimming pool proper are least popular because the great volume of water in the pool tends to absorb and blunt the force of the incoming water. Thus agitation is limited to the immediate vicinity of the inlets. The temperature of the incoming water is that of the pool water.

But if you build an alcove off the pool or put in a separate pool, water agitation is more pronounced—as in a hydrotherapy tank at an Easter Seal rehab center—because the volume of water in the therapy pool is small. Furthermore, the water temperature can be raised.

The dimensions of alcoves and separate pools are variable; but for best water movement, width and length should generally not exceed 6 ft. Water depth should be between 20 and 24 in. This is deep enough for an adult to sit on the bottom of the pool with his chin above water level. If the pool is to be used also by children, the depth might be decreased; but for long-run use, it is wiser to let them sit on concrete blocks placed in the pool as temporary benches or to install around the sides of the pool a rope they can hang on.

In an alcove installation, a wall slightly higher than the water level of the main pool separates the two pools. This confines the agitation to the therapy pool but permits the water entering this pool to spill over into the main pool. Thus the water in the two pools is mixed, and the main pool indirectly keeps the therapy pool clean. In a completely separate therapy pool, this is impossible.

Regardless of whether you put in an alcove pool or a separate pool, the most economical way to agitate and heat it is to use the pump, filter and heater for the swimming pool proper. All you need is a valve, or system of valves, which permits you to circulate either the swimming-pool water or the therapy-pool water through the filter and heater. The swimming-pool plumbing, as in any pool, consists of a main drain line and one or more return lines. Similarly, the therapy-pool plumbing consists of a drain line and a return line with one to three jet inlets. A small pipe extending above ground introduces air into the therapy pool return line to aerate the water.

When the therapy pool is in use, the valves controlling the plumbing for that pool are opened and those controlling the swimming-pool plumbing are closed. Water from the therapy pool is then drawn into the pump, circulated through the filter and heater and returned to the therapy pool.

To raise the therapy pool water to a higher temperature than the swimming-pool water, the pool heater should be equipped with a control which allows you to switch quickly from the preset swimming temperature of, say, 78° to a preset therapy temperature of, say, 100°. The alternatives are to install a separate heater for the therapy pool or to add small auxiliary heaters on the return line to the pool.

Lifesaving Equipment Your choice is between a light-weight aluminum life pole and a life buoy. The former should be at least 10 ft. long, and some localities require that it incorporate a large shepherd's crook at the end. But the problem I have found with any such pole is that it doesn't stay stored (usually hanging in U-shaped hooks on the pool fence) where it should. There is some fascination in light-weight poles that causes people to use them for all kinds of things the poles are not supposed to be used for.

Life buoys should be at least 20 in. in diameter and tied securely to a sturdy polyethylene rope at least as long at the pool. They are usually hung on a fence or a special standard at the back edge of the deck.

Lifelines In my old gunite pool, a strong, ½-in. polyethylene rope runs around the entire pool (except at the shallow-end steps) several inches below the coping. I view it as a mixed blessing. Its main drawback is that, if the water level is a little low, the rope traps much of the surface debris. On the other hand, it is the only positive handhold around the pool, since the coping is improperly shaped. It provides perfect support when you practice kicking and take leg exercises. And long before my grandchildren learned to swim, the rope was the something they needed to hang on to while they lost their fear of the water. Even now I can see the triumphant look on Siobhan's face as she made a complete circle of the pool by grabbing the rope, leaning back and "walking" around the walls. It was no time at all after that that she began to swim.

Lifelines of this sort are rare, however. In fact, I question whether they could be used in any pool other than one with concrete walls, because the strain on them may be great. But lifelines strung across the pool at the point where the bottom plunges downward are quite common and eminently worthwhile if there are non-swimmers in the family.

The line may be made of polyethylene with or without a few plastic floats; or it may be a continuous line of plastic floats threaded on a stainless-steel cable. The latter is similar to the long lines used to mark racing lanes. For convenience in attaching and detaching the line to the eye bolts in the pool walls, it should have brass rope hooks at the ends.

Alarm Systems An automatic alarm system which warns when someone or something is in your pool is a desirable accessory, particularly if the pool is distant from the house. Theoretically, of course, you should not need it if your pool is properly fenced. But even in spite of fences, people and animals sometimes fall into pools and get in trouble when no one is available to go to their rescue. And, often, unauthorized swimmers sneak in over a fence.

Pool-alarm systems now on the market are designed to blow a horn or ring a bell the instant they detect the presence of a body in the pool. They work in three ways.

One system employs a sonarlike sensor placed on the bottom of a pool. This sounds an alarm when it picks up the sound of something entering the pool.

Another system has a tape which is pasted to the sides of the pool just under the coping. Ripples or splashing water striking this set off the alarm.

A third system made by several firms has sensing devices installed in a float which bobs around on the surface of the pool or is anchored in one place. Like the tape, it is activated by moving water.

In most alarm systems, regardless of design, the signal is carried from the sensor by wires to the alarm, which may be located close to or even inside the house. But at least one system has wireless transmission. And in another case, the alarm and sensor are combined in an aerosol unit which floats around the pool.

Except for the aerosol device, all alarms are battery operated, which means you must check them occasionally to make sure they are still in operating order. This is a minor disadvantage. Another disadvantage of every alarm system is that you must remember to turn it off when you go swimming and turn it on again when you leave the pool.

Cost of the systems ranges from $60–$240.

Pool Covers

I don't have a cover for my pool because I like to refill it every spring with fresh water and have a sufficient supply to do this; so it doesn't make any difference how dirty the pool gets over winter.

And I am not at all sure that my friends Betty and Hudson have a cover either; but if they don't, it's for quite a different reason. Several years ago, Betty was awakened one winter morning by strange noises coming from the direction of their pool. Looking out the window, she saw a horse floundering in the water. Somehow he had walked out on the pool cover; the cover had given way under his hooves; and there he was hanging in the cover up to his flanks in the water—a very unhappy animal.

"Well, he won't drown," Betty assured Hudson; and he replied, "We ought to be able to get him out in short order." But those proved to be nothing more than brave words. As the morning wore on and the neighborhood experts and owner of the horse assembled to give advice, one thing after another was done to haul the beast to safety—and nothing worked. If he had fallen into an uncovered pool, he would have swum to the shallow end, where he had footing, and could then have been helped up over the wall. But here he was trapped—helpless—like a child in a canvas swing suspended too far off the ground for him to put his feet down.

Eventually Hudson gave into the inevitable. With a knife tied to a pole, he slit the cover in two so the horse could swim; and a strange incident was brought to its conclusion. So was the pool cover.

In other words, not everyone wants—or needs—a pool cover. Therefore, since a good cover costs several hundred dollars, you should consider carefully the purposes a cover serves and whether these are important to you.

The principal purpose is to keep debris out of the pool and discourage the growth of algae in winter, and so make for easier clean-up in the spring.

A second purpose is to keep a pool free of dirt and algae in the summer, and simultaneously to reduce the loss of water through evaporation and cut the loss of heat from the water at night (see Chapter 10). But because most covers are heavy and cumbersome, few pool owners use them in this way.

The third purpose of a cover is to keep children, grownups and animals from falling into a pool. But here again it must be remembered that a cover is effective only if it is so easy to handle that it is pulled over the pool whenever the pool is not in use. (It is significant that building codes do not permit a pool cover to be used as a substitute for a fence around the pool.)

Several types of pool cover are available.

Inexpensive covers of plastic mesh are of little value. I bought one once to keep our garden pool clean; but it was a failure, for although it kept out leaves from the two oaks overhanging the pool it let through bushels of acorns, twigs, insects and other smallish particles of dirt.

Another type of cover looks like a solid sheet of plastic fabric but actually allows rain and snow water to drip through. The result is a mixed blessing. As a barrier to dirt, the cover is excellent; and it also does an excellent job of discouraging algae and preventing heat loss. But it does allow a pool to fill with water in winter, thus threatening the coping and upper walls with damage.

The best of the sheetlike covers is made of opaque, solid vinyl which keeps everything, including water, out of a pool. But because it is water-tight, special steps must be taken in winter to keep it from being weighted down into the pool by the water accumulating on the surface. One way of doing this is to toss into the pool, before it is covered, one or two big, buoyant plastic "pillows" which hold the cover higher in the middle than around the edges. The other solution is to place on the cover near the middle a tiny submersible electric pump which removes the water as it accumulates. To keep rainwater from seeping into the pool from under the sides of the cover, the best covers are tied to anchors installed in the deck or driven into the ground around the deck. They are then weighted down with water poured into sleeves formed in the four edges of the cover.

(Note that in order to seal out dirt completely with either kind of solid cover you must remove the ladder from the pool so the cover can be stretched tight over the coping on all sides. Slides, diving stands and any other equipment built into the deck close to the pool may also have to be removed.)

Motorized pool covers are the most elaborate and expensive available; but because they operate automatically, they are useful in all seasons and for all purposes. One type of cover consists of a solid sheet of plastic fabric which slides in tracks fastened to the sides of the pool just below the coping. A motor pulls the cover out flat over the pool when the pool is not in use, and then draws it back into a bundle under the diving board when the pool is occupied.

Another kind of motorized cover is made of two giant, rigid panels of aluminum and fiberglass which lie across the pool longitudinally when it is unoccupied. When you want to go swimming, a touch of a button causes the panels to lift up and glide back high above the deck on either side of the pool, where they serve as sunshades.

10 Heating the Pool

I'm no polar bear. On October 10, 1972, when the temperature of the water in my pool dipped overnight from 60° to 56° and the daytime air temperature, which had been running in the 70's, dropped into the 50's, I quit swimming for the year.

But my neighbor, Park, kept right on going—at least on days when the air temperature was benign. Park keeps his swimming pool heated to 85°.

Statistics indicate that in recent years better than 50 per cent of all new pool owners, like Park, installed water heaters. The reason: For relatively low initial cost—roughly 10 per cent of the price of the pool itself—they can increase pool use substantially. In fact, heating propagandists claim usage is increased fully 50 per cent. But the figure is difficult to substantiate.

The hard facts are these:

With a heated pool you *can* swim more hours of the day throughout the swimming season, although no one knows how many people actually have the time and inclination to do so. And if you have a heated swimming-pool enclosure, you *can* swim the year 'round. These, in other words, are possibilities.

The actualities are that, with a heated pool, you start swimming earlier in the spring, continue swimming later in the fall, and enjoy a more equable, salubrious water temperature at all times.

The Dynamics of Pool Heating

It is no mystery that the temperature of a swimming pool rises and falls with the temperature of the air. Although the two figures are identical only occasionally—and then only briefly—during the warm seasons of the year, they are in general equilibrium. This means that if you want to know what the temperature of your pool usually runs in the spring, summer and fall, all you have to do is look up the normal mean air temperatures for these months.

For example, despite the fact that I check the temperature of my pool every day during the swimming season, my idea of how it averages out during any given month is imprecise because I have never taken the trouble to write the readings down. But by consulting statistics supplied by the nearest Weather Bureau station, which happens to be in New Haven, I find the normal air temperatures for the season are as follows:

April	47°
May	57°
June	66°
July	72°
August	71°
September	64°
October	54°

Experience and memory tell me that this is a pretty accurate record of my pool temperature. I start swimming along about May 15, when the water reaches 60°, and stop along about mid-October. But I am not really comfortable until the water temperature hits about 70° late in June. And I am not positively blissful until it runs 75°–80° for a few days in midsummer.

I make no claim to being the typical swimmer, but most people react in more or less the same way. The favorite water temperature of American swimmers is somewhere between 75° and 82°. There are some, of course, who prefer it lower; and others who like it higher. (People with arthritis may heat their pools as high as 95°.) But if you want to pin down to a single figure, 78° is about perfect by most standards. This is also the temperature which the Red Cross recommends as being most healthful and safe.

What this means is clear: I should have a pool heater, not just to extend the swimming season but so I can swim more happily throughout the summer.

More important, it helps to explain charts published by swimming-pool-heater manufacturers which show that there are relatively few communities in the United States where you don't "need" a pool heater during the summer, and that there are no communities outside Hawaii where you don't "need" a pool heater at some time during the entire year. Such charts are based on (1) normal monthly air temperatures recorded by the Weather Bureau and (2) the assumption that when air and water temperature falls below 78°, water heating is called for.

But What Does It Cost? Compelling as the argument in favor of pool heaters may be, the cost of operation is a question which worries everyone—even the firms that sell the fuel. Too many people who have put in heaters have had such distressingly expensive experiences that they shut the heaters down; and they make no efforts to conceal their irritation. Their reaction is understandable, although it might be said that they have only themselves to blame for not looking into matters more carefully in the first place.

This, however, is not so easily done. Solid information about pool-heating costs is scarce. This is partly because most people use the same fuel for pool-heating as for house-heating and domestic water-heating; consequently, they cannot apportion costs accurately. But the main difficulty is that no two pools are identical or are heated in identical fashion. Cost of pool-heating depends on the size of the pool, its location, the climate, the fuel, the heater, how the pool is used, when it is heated and to what temperature.

The most authoritative information comes from the San Diego Gas & Electric Co. as a result of extensive research done by the firm several years ago. On the basis of this, it prepared a table showing how much it costs to heat a typical San Diego pool with 500 sq. ft. of surface area if the heater runs 12 hours every day. The table, which I have expanded to show normal mean air temperatures in San Diego, is reproduced here:

Typical Fuel Costs

	MEAN AIR TEMPERATURE	POOL TEMPERATURE				
		75°	78°	80°	82°	85°
January	55°	$ 26	$ 34	$ 41	$ 50	$ 66
February	56°	23	32	38	46	63
March	59°	19	26	31	38	51
April	62°	17	24	29	35	46
May	64°	15	18	22	27	40
June	66°	12	15	18	22	29
July	70°	4	6	8	11	15
August	72°	2	3	4	5	7
September	70°	3	5	6	7	9
October	66°	13	18	22	27	35
November	62°	20	28	34	41	54
December	57°	22	30	36	44	59
ANNUAL COSTS		$176	$239	$289	$353	$474

Admittedly, the table applies specifically to San Diego. But if you live in a similar climate and have a similar gas rate—8 cents

This 18-by-38 ft. pool in southern Connecticut is heated by the pool heater shown at right with the pool pump and filter. (All of the equipment is installed in the right end of the poolhouse.) The heater burns bottled gas. In 1972, when the heater was operated continuously from June 10 to December 5, the cost of fuel came to almost exactly $650. If the pool had been spot-heated instead, the cost could have been reduced substantially.

per therm (100,000 Btu's)—the figures can be applied to your own pool. If your pool is larger or smaller than 500 sq. ft., add or subtract 20 per cent to the dollar figures for each 100 sq. ft. of difference in the pool area.

If you live in a totally different climate, compare your normal mean monthly air temperatures with those for San Diego. Where the temperatures are similar, the heating costs should also be reasonably close (assuming that your gas utility's rates are the same as San Diego's). For example, if your normal mean temperature for May is 57°, you can figure that the cost of heating your pool in that month is about the same as the cost of heating a San Diego pool in December.

If you live in a different climate and use an oil-fired pool heater, pick out the San Diego dollar figures for the months with temperatures corresponding to yours, divide each of them by .08 and add five zeros to the answer. This gives you the approximate number of Btu's (British thermal units) required for heating in San Diego. Then divide by 140,000 to find how many gallons of oil would be consumed, and multiply by the price you pay for oil. For example, if it costs $30 to heat a San Diego pool in December, dividing .08 into $30.00 and adding five zeros gives an answer of 37,500,000 Btu's. Dividing this figure by 140,000 reveals that you would burn roughly 270 gal. of oil to heat a pool of similar size in any month with a mean air temperature of 57°. At 20 cents a gallon, your heating bill would be $54.

The value of San Diego Gas & Electric's research is not, however, limited to these dollar figures. The research also produced some important recommendations for heating *all* pools economically:

(1) Make sure you can be happy only at the high-water temperature you think you need. For each 1-degree decrease in temperature, you lower the heating cost 10 per cent or more.

Once the entire family is satisfied with the pool temperature, don't let anyone other than the head of the household touch the temperature control. When everyone has a finger in the pie, fuel bills usually rise.

(2) Make sure the temperature control on the heater is calibrated accurately. If the control is set for 75° but actually lets the water reach 76°, heating cost is increased 10 per cent. The San Diego researchers found that it was not at all uncommon for temperature controls to be as much as eight degrees out of cali-

bration. At that rate you would be paying approximately 80 per cent more for fuel than you should.

To check the temperature control, find the temperature of the water in the pool with an accurate immersion-bulb thermometer. Then, if the heater is not running, turn the control slowly toward a higher setting until it goes on. Note the ignition temperature and continue turning the control to a point 5 degrees above ignition. Let the heater run for a minute to allow pool water to reach the temperature control; then turn the control down slowly until the heater shuts off again. The temperature of the dial setting and that of the pool water should now agree. If they do not, have the dealer or utility calibrate the control correctly.

(3) Cover the pool at night to prevent excess heat loss. A light-weight black polyethylene sheet will reduce fuel requirements as much as 25–30 per cent. A heavy pool cover is even more effective.

Of course, the problem with pool covers other than those which are mechanized is that they are awkward to handle and you usually need a helper to pull them over the pool. But you can make it an easy, quick, one-man operation if you take a tip from a pool owner I know in western Connecticut. He rolls his heavy vinyl

To conserve heat and prevent growth of algae in the indoor pool illustrated in Chapter 14, the owner covers it when it is not in use with a sheet of heavy vinyl rolled around a 6-in.-diameter aluminum tube (background). The cover can be opened or closed by one person in about two minutes.

cover up on a pool-spanning, 6-in. aluminum tube of the type used to carry conduits in large buildings. He can roll the cover out over the pool from one end to the other—and back again—with his foot.

(4) Above all, don't try to maintain the same water temperature 24 hours a day every day of the swimming season. This consumes considerably more fuel than spot-heating—heating the pool only when you intend to use it.

Spot-heating requires that you put the heater on a time clock. If the pump and filter are on a time clock and are set to operate no more than 12 hours a day, the same clock can be used for the heater. But if filter operation exceeds 12 hours, a second time clock should be installed for the heater.

If you normally start swimming after 10 a.m., you should set the clock to turn the heater on every day at about 6 a.m. (The exact starting time depends on the season of the year, how much the water temperature usually drops at night when unheated, and whether your heater is sized to raise the water temperature one-half or one degree per hour.) By the time you're ready to leap off the diving board, the water should be up to the temperature you like.

On the other hand, if you are accustomed to taking an early-morning dip, you should set the heater to turn on at about 11 the night before.

Similarly, if you swim only on weekends, you should—depending on the season and heater size—turn the heater on 24 to 48 hours before swimming hour. But even in this extreme case, you would save money by spot-heating.

Whatever the turn-on time, the heater should be turned off about an hour before the last swimmer climbs out of the pool.

Types of Pool Heater   Pool heaters operate on natural or bottled gas, oil and electricity. At present, however, electric heaters are not very common because of generally high operating costs.

Most heaters in use are compact rectangular or cylindrical units which are installed on the return line between the filter and the pool. In some, the water passing through is heated directly by the flame. These are called direct heaters, and cost in the neighborhood of $450–$650. In others, the water is heated as it passes through a chamber filled with boiling hot water or steam. These are indirect heaters, or heat-exchange models, and are priced somewhat higher.

90

Both are designed to operate only when the pump and filter are going.

In buying either type of heater, the main points to be checked are whether provisions have been made (1) to control the excessive condensation which is a problem in pool heaters because of its corrosive effect; (2) to minimize the formation of scale inside the heaters; and (3) to protect the heaters against the corrosive chemicals in the pool water.

In another completely different type of heating system, used infrequently in concrete pools, pool-water temperature is raised by circulating hot water through copper tubing embedded in the bottom and sides of the pool. This is called radiant heating and is exactly like the system which was fleetingly popular in houses built in the fifties. Pool water is heated more evenly than with other systems, and there are no corrosion or scaling problems. But the system must be custom-designed to each pool and is expensive to install. It is also slow to respond when heat is called for; and if a leak develops, murder!

A fourth heating system, which excites imagination but is rarely used, is solar heating. In this, pool water is heated as it

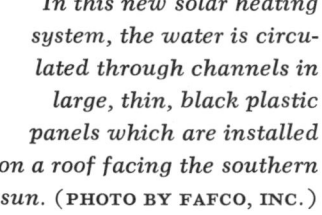

In this new solar heating system, the water is circulated through channels in large, thin, black plastic panels which are installed on a roof facing the southern sun. (PHOTO BY FAFCO, INC.)

circulates through long coils of copper or black plastic tubing which is usually mounted on the house roof, where it is exposed to the southern sun. The principal advantage of this system is that there is no fuel cost. Additionally, if it is operated at night, it can be used to cool the pool. But unfortunately, it is fully effective only in areas with steady, intense sunlight, such as California and the Southwest. Even there, efficiency drops in bad weather and in winter.

Solar-heating systems have generally been homemade, although a few firms sell prefab systems. The newest and most promising of the latter is a Redwood City, California, company which channels pool water through black plastic panels resembling a slab of plywood. For spring-to-fall heating, the total area of the panels should be half of the pool area. The cost of panels plus a thermostatic control for a 500-sq.-ft. pool is approximately $540. To use a pool in cool weather, you would need additional panels or a supplementary heater.

Sizing Direct and Indirect Pool Heaters

Selecting the proper-size heater for a swimming pool should not be a concern of the pool owner. It's a technical problem which should be left to the pool builder or dealer. Experience has proved, however, that these "experts" often install undersized heaters in the belief that these will hold down fuel costs as well as original cost. The actual result is quite different. True, the initial cost of the heater is low. But fuel costs soar because, in order to maintain the desired water temperature, the heaters must operate almost constantly.

To realize the 30-to-40-per-cent savings accruing from spot-heating, you need a big heater which can bring pool water quickly up to temperature.

Pool-heater manufacturers and their dealers use several methods of sizing heaters. But the commonest and easiest method is one developed by the Commercial Water Heating Subcommittee of the American Gas Association. It is designed to permit selection of a heater which will raise the water in an in-ground pool to a desired temperature in a 24-hour period. It is applicable to heaters burning any fuel.

First, determine the surface area of your pool in square feet. Decide on the temperature you want to keep the water. Then look up the mean air temperature for the coldest month during which you expect to swim and subtract this from the desired water temperature. The heater size, stated in Btu-per-hour input, is then easy to find in the table below.

Water-Heater Sizing Chart for In-ground Pools

POOL AREA (sq. ft.)	BTU/HR. INPUT TEMPERATURE DIFFERENTIAL BETWEEN AIR AND POOL WATER				
	10°F.	15°F.	20°F.	25°F.	30°F.
200	56,000	84,000	112,000	140,000	168,000
300	84,000	126,000	168,000	210,000	252,000
400	112,000	168,000	224,000	280,000	336,000
500	140,000	210,000	280,000	350,000	420,000
600	168,000	252,000	336,000	420,000	503,000
700	196,000	294,000	392,000	490,000	587,000
800	224,000	336,000	447,000	559,000	671,000
900	252,000	377,000	503,000	629,000	755,000
1,000	280,000	419,000	559,000	699,000	839,000
1,200	336,000	503,000	671,000	839,000	1,007,000
1,400	392,000	587,000	783,000	979,000	1,174,000

The figures given can be adjusted to meet special requirements. For example, if the average wind velocity across your pool is 10 mph instead of the 3.5 on which the table is based, multiply the heater input by 1.5. If you plan to use electricity rather than gas or oil for fuel, multiply the input figure by 0.8 after applying the wind velocity factor. If heat-up time is not important and you are interested only in *maintaining* water temperature, multiply the input figure by 0.6 after applying the wind velocity factor. If the average depth of your pool is more or less than 5½ ft., add or subtract 10 per cent to the input figure for each foot of variance in depth.

Above-ground pools outdoors require larger heaters. Pools in heated enclosures use smaller.

Cooling a Pool Unpleasantly warm pool water is a problem only in our warmest climates; but there it is for many people a very real problem. Unfortunately, there is no good solution.

Drawing off part of the warm water and adding fresh cold water is a possibility but not a very practical one unless you happen to own a spring or well with an almost inexhaustible supply.

Another possibility is to shade the pool at least during the heat of the day. This is often done in Florida by building a screen-wire enclosure completely around the pool (it also keeps out insects). Or you can simply erect over the pool a network of sturdy wires and pull a canvas awning out over this.

To lower the temperature of the water in this Florida pool in the summer, water from the filter returns through a perforated pipe from which it spurts out over the pool in tiny streams.

A third idea invented by one of my ingenious friends is to pipe the return water from the filter through a long pipe mounted along one side of the pool. The pipe is perforated at about 18-in. intervals on the pool side and the water spurts from these holes out over the pool. Thus it is cooled slightly by air and evaporation.

A fourth solution, mentioned earlier in this chapter, is to install a solar heating system.

94

11 Lighting and Wiring in and Around the Pool

Lighting the swimming pool not only allows you to swim into the wee hours of the night but also adds immeasurably to the beauty of your garden. You can hardly expect happier results from a relatively small investment.

Ideally, lights should be installed both in the pool and around it. This gives you greater flexibility in creating lighted settings to suit your needs and moods. But area lighting alone and underwater lighting alone have value.

Area lighting helps to keep people from falling into the pool and also keeps them from stumbling over furnishings, equipment and plantings near the pool. It is necessary to entertaining. And it gives plants a twice-to-be-enjoyed beauty: You see them growing naturally around the sides of the pool, and you see them again mirrored in the dark water.

Underwater lighting also contributes to safety, but in a somewhat different way. It not only keeps people from falling into the pool but also guards them against danger once they're in. If one of a group happens to fall in, the rest can see instantly where he is and go to his rescue. In addition, the light helps to prevent divers from banging into the bottom of the pool.

More than this, underwater lighting gives a pool a glowing charm which has a strangely magnetic appeal when you are nearby. It has something of the feeling of a jewel displayed on black velvet. But somewhat surprisingly, this appeal disappears as you move away from the pool unless the area around it is also lighted. Seen from a distance, a pool which is lighted only from inside is an oddity—an unreality which makes the whole scene unreal.

How to Light Your Pool Underwater

Underwater lighting is most easily installed when a pool is under construction. It can, however, be put in as an afterthought, although this is rather difficult, especially in concrete pools.

Two kinds of underwater lights are made. So-called dry-niche lights are designed for use in a cavity constructed in the side of the pool and sealed off from the water. Wet-niche lights are submersible units. They are also installed in a cavity but with water all around them. The latter are in most common use because they

A delightful nighttime setting for swimming. Lights directed upward from the ground bring out the beautiful branch structure and open foliage of a weeping birch. (PHOTO BY WESTINGHOUSE)

are easy to pull out for relamping (with a dry-niche light you must lower the pool level).

Whichever type of light is used, it must be constructed of sturdy, corrosion-proof materials, be sealed against leaks and be designed so the bulb can be readily replaced.

The size and number of lights installed is largely a matter of personal choice. In residential pools the usual practice is to provide 0.75 watts per sq. ft. of water surface. However, if a pool is used by a sizable number of very active or competitive swimmers, it is wise to increase the wattage, as in public pools, to as much as 3 watts per sq. ft. In other words, if you have a 20-by-40-ft. pool, you should install anywhere from 600 to 2,400 watts of light. The lamps used for the purpose are normally PAR sealed bulbs made of tough tempered glass and rated at 300, 400, 500 or 1,000 watts.

Most home pools have only a single light, which is installed 18–24 in. below the water line at the end of the pool under the diving board. If two or more lights are required, they are installed in one of the side walls at the same depth. At the deep end of the pool, the lights should be spaced 12–18 ft. from one another and from the end wall. In the shallow end (in water less than 5 ft. deep), the spacing can be increased to 15–20 ft.

An important point to be considered in locating lights in a pool is the glare they create. Even though they should be aimed slightly downward, the glare off the water surface is considerable. Consequently, you should be careful not to locate the lights so they will shine toward the place from which you are most likely to view the pool at night. This means that if your pool is close to the house, you should not put the lights in the wall facing the house. Similarly, don't put lights in a wall facing the deck area on which you usually relax. (On the other hand, never put lights in the wall facing a diving board.)

An additional way to cope with the glare of an underwater light is to install a dimmer control so you can adjust the intensity of the light to suit your activities. If the pool is not in use, lower the light level until the water emits just a soft glow. Then increase the light when you are ready for a brisk game of water polo.

With the underwater lights on, the bottom of this pool is clearly visible; when they're off, the pool becomes a black mirror reflecting the trees in the background. One drawback of this lighting installation and of that on page is that, because the lights are at ground level, they tend to attract insects too close to the pool. (PHOTOS BY GENERAL ELECTRIC)

How to Light the Area Around the Pool

If you don't have underwater lighting, the only way you can make your pool completely safe for nighttime swimming is to floodlight it from all sides. Illuminating engineers call for one 150-watt floodlamp for each 45 sq. ft. of water surface. The lamps should be mounted on 12–15 ft. poles placed 6 ft. from the edges of the pool. Unfortunately, such an installation is guaranteed to turn your lovely garden into a visual atrocity, alienate your neighbors for life and attract bugs by the millions.

In the circumstances, you may prefer to compromise safety for livability.

One of the first swimming pools I lighted was a big one (without an underwater light) within full view of the house but a good 250 ft. from it. The owners were terrified that someone might drown unseen; but at the same time, they wanted to retain the natural beauty of the setting. So after some experimentation, I installed two floodlights in bullet reflectors high in a tree at one end of the pool. A 150-watt lamp was aimed into the crown of a handsome old sycamore at the opposite end of the pool. A 75-watt lamp was directed down on some small deciduous trees just behind the pool.

All our objectives were achieved. From the house you could see anyone falling into the pool, although there was not enough light in the pool to make rescue easy. Swimmers had light to see what they were doing, yet they could not look directly into the source of the light. The entire pool area took on a simple but theatrical quality when seen either from the house or the pool deck. And the bugs were no more troublesome than they had been before the lights were put in.

A 300-watt underwater light is installed in the shallow end of the pool but is hidden from the camera by a floating chair. This is an unusual location for such a light but was in this case necessary to direct the glare away from the house. Subdued lights on the house walls give adequate illumination on the deck. (PHOTO BY GENERAL ELECTRIC)

Establishing objectives is the first step in lighting the area around a pool. The list you draw up almost certainly will include those above. In addition, you may want to provide light for such things as entertaining, barbecuing and playing poolside games.

The second step is to round up all your outdoor extension cords and start experimenting with the placement of lights. (But make sure the ground and plants are dry. And don't carry lights and wires around while they are energized; put them in place before turning on the current.)

The rules to be followed in lighting around the pool and the methods employed are no different from those for lighting any other garden area:

(1) Don't try to turn night into day by using a great deal of light. For one thing, there is beauty in darkness—a magic that is easily destroyed by large wattages. For another thing, you need surprisingly little light to see where you are going and to keep from stumbling into the pool. (But note once again that area lighting will not illuminate the depths of a pool unless it includes a battery of floodlights. That's why it is advisable to install underwater lighting as well as area lighting.)

(2) Take care not to let any lights shine into neighboring properties or into your own windows.

(3) Conceal all light sources. Even a small bulb can be blinding; and the bright spot of light is anything but pretty.

True, concealing bulbs sometimes takes a bit of doing; but tree trunks and limbs, foliage and clumps of flowers generally provide many excellent hiding places. In addition, you can hide bulbs in hooded fixtures, tin cans, flower pots, hollow building tiles—anything that happens to be appropriate to that particular part of the pool area.

(4) In the immediate vicinity of the pool use white light only. It brings out the color of foliage, flowers, paving, etc., better than colored light; and because white is the color we associate with light, it is less disturbing than colored light.

Furthermore, since your pool may be painted green or blue, it glows green or blue if it has an underwater light. White light around the pool looks better with this than colored light.

(5) To avoid an onslaught of insects, try to install all lights high off the ground or at a distance from the pool. As a further precaution, install a blue light or an electric insect trap equipped with a special BL lamp as far from the pool as possible. These have such a powerful appeal for insects that they will lure them away from the white lights.

The actual way in which you use lights around a pool depends on the way the area has been developed and planted. In all cases, the pool is the focal point. This is especially true if it has an underwater light; but even if it doesn't, the eye is drawn to it instantly by the reflections on its glassy surface. For this reason, all lighting around the pool must be subordinate to the pool. At the same time, it must be visually linked with the pool. You should not try to make a permanent feature of some other element in the area, because it will then compete with the pool for attention and thus destroy the unity of the scene. This does not mean, however, that you cannot on occasion concentrate light on, say, the poolhouse or a special games area if you want that to be the temporary focus of attention.

The trees in the pool area should be the first things you light. Pick out one or two which have especially attractive structures or foliage and concentrate on them. If they are reasonably far from the pool, lighting them from the bottom up will create the most dramatic effect and will not cause an insect problem at the poolside. Simply place the lights on the ground or in the lower limbs and aim up. Trees growing near the pool, however, should be lighted from the top down. This creates a moonlight effect on the ground below while keeping the insects off the ground. The alternative is to direct light into the trees from lamps installed in nearby trees or on the roof of the poolhouse.

Whether you light a tree from above or below, you usually need only one floodlamp if it is placed close to the center of the tree. But when you light a tree from the side, you need two lights aimed from different angles in order to reveal the entire tree and avoid a flat look. For best results, one light should be stronger than the other.

Shrubs are generally lighted from below. The most effective are those with an open branching structure and not-too-dense foliage. Bamboo, blueberry and *euonymus alatus* are examples. These are especially attractive when silhouetted against a lighted wall or solid fence.

Flowers, on the other hand, are much more difficult to light. The plants do not have very interesting shapes, so the only reason to light them is to bring out the color of the blossoms. But if you use too much light, it tends to wash out the color. And if you use just a little light—25 watts may be enough—the fixture must be so close to the flowers that it will attract bugs to the vicinity.

The fence or wall around the pool area may also present problems if you light them deliberately (to use as a background) or if they happen to be struck by light aimed at plants. For one thing, wire fences are no better looking at night than during the day— and they may look worse. But even a beautiful fence or wall becomes a detriment if it is close to the pool, because under light its closeness is emphasized and the pool area feels small and confining.

Happily, you can avoid this situation either by leaving the wall in darkness or by lighting it and then installing lights in the garden behind it to give depth to the scene.

How to Make the Electrical Installation Safe

All electrical equipment installed near a swimming pool is a potential hazard. This includes not only the underwater and above-ground lights but also the pump motor, time clock, motor-operated pool cover, automatic pool-cleaning equipment, electric water heater, appliances in the poolhouse, and power tools and appliances used around the pool.

Because of the hazard, some communities require that lights be operated at 12 volts. But even here 120 or 240 volts are required for other purposes; and at these voltages, equipment and wiring can be lethal if not installed properly by an expert who obeys the local electrical code and good common-sense rules.

To begin with, all permanent wiring within 10 ft. of the pool must be installed underground; and for the sake of appearances, if nothing else, it should also be underground outside this area. Even though flexible direct-burial cable may be permitted in your community, it is a good idea to run the wires through somewhat over-sized rigid conduits so that if you want to change the lighting around the pool or add electrical equipment, you will not have to tear up the deck in order to install new wiring.

If your electrical usage at the pool is substantial, you will need several wiring circuits. The pool pump should be installed on its own 20-amp., 120-volt circuit. A 20-amp., 120-volt circuit is required for the operation of small appliances and tools; and if you have a kitchen in the poolhouse, you will require separate 20-amp. circuits for most of the large appliances. In addition, you will need one or more circuits for the lighting installation. The exact number depends on the total wattage of the lights, the amperage at which the circuits are fused, the size of the wire in the circuits and the distance from the fuse box to the farthest light. To illustrate: If you have a 15-amp. circuit with No. 14 wire, it will carry a load of no more than 1,800 watts. At this wattage the circuit must not exceed 40 ft. in length; but if you reduce the wattage to 1,000, the circuit length can be increased to 70 ft. On the other hand, if you have a 20-amp. circuit with No. 12 wire, it will carry a maximum load of 2,400 watts; and the circuit can be 50 ft. long.

For safety and convenience, all circuits should be controlled by switches installed at some logical, easy-to-get-at point within the pool area. It is also advisable to have a switch for at least one of the lighting circuits inside your house so you don't have to grope your way to the pool and so you can see what is going on at the pool if you suddenly hear splashing.

Outlets used for appliances, tools and plug-in lamps must be installed at least 10 ft. from the pool; and lighting outlets, switches and junction boxes should be at least 5 ft. from the pool. This is to keep them out of arm's reach of people in the pool or standing in puddles around the edges. All such equipment, as well as light fixtures, must be of waterproof construction to prevent entrance of rain, snow and water splashed from the pool.

To avoid any possibility that leaves will become trapped next to lightbulbs and catch fire, lighting fixtures which are aimed upward should be covered with wire mesh or glass lenses. And to prevent lightbulbs from shattering on the pool deck when struck by water, never use ordinary bulbs in large sizes unless they are in completely enclosed fixtures. The safest bulbs are the unbreakable (unless you drop them) PAR type. Household bulbs of 25 watts or less are also usually safe, because they don't generate much heat and can therefore survive exposure to moisture.

The most important safety measures you should take, however, involve proper grounding of all electrical equipment in and around the pool and the installation of a new device known as a ground fault circuit interrupter, or simply, a GFI.

Electrical equipment is grounded by using three wires rather than two in cords and cables. The third wire runs from the exposed metal housing of, say, the pool pump motor to a metal rod buried in the ground below the fuse box. If for some reason the motor housing should become energized, the ground wire allows the current to flow to the ground; the circuit becomes overloaded, and the fuse blows.

Normally equipment which is grounded is safe. But sometimes something goes wrong with the grounding system. Then if the motor housing becomes energized and you happen to touch it while standing on a wet pool deck, you'll get a shock. And unfortunately, it doesn't have to be much of a shock to be fatal. A healthy man can be killed if only 60/1,000 of an ampere of current passes through his chest for one second. This is about equal to the current used by a 7½-watt Christmas-tree bulb.

Leakages such as this are called ground faults. So, as the name implies, ground-fault circuit interrupters are designed to detect leakages and cut off the power before it can do any harm. Models currently available respond to ground-fault currents of as little as 2/1,000 to 5/1,000 of an ampere; and they can break the circuit in a tiny fraction of a second.

Because experience has proved that small appliances, electric tools and portable lights are the foremost cause of electrical accidents around swimming pools, the 1971 National Electrical Code stipulates that all outlets between 10 and 15 ft. of an in-ground pool into which such equipment is plugged must be protected by a GFI. In addition, underwater lights must be protected by GFI's if other adequate measures are not taken to keep them from being hazardous.

Similar protection for other electrical equipment in the area around in-ground pools is not required by the code, but according to people who helped to draw up the code, this is likely to change. "All electrical devices installed or used near a pool can be dangerous," one expert told me. "For example, if the piping between the pool and the pump and filter is plastic—as it almost always is—it is possible for current to leak from a faulty pump into the pool. So it is really wise to protect the pump motor by a GFI, too.

"It's our feeling that other electrical equipment should be protected in the same way. In fact, to be completely safe, everything electrical within the vicinity of a swimming pool should be hooked up to a ground-fault circuit interrupter.* And when I say 'vicinity,' I don't just mean within 15 ft. of the pool. It's amazing what long extension cords people use to bring radios and barbecues and hair dryers to the poolside."

But the cost?

A ground-fault circuit interrupter which is large enough to protect only the outlets near a pool costs roughly $35. A unit which will protect an extensive electrical installation costs $125. That's hardly too much to pay for safety.

---

* The National Electrical Code also requires that "all electrical equipment used with storable (above-ground) swimming pools shall be supplied by circuits protected by ground fault circuit interrupters."

12 Developing the Surroundings

Since your family will undoubtedly spend more time around the pool than in it, you should lavish equal attention on the development of this area. Even if you can't afford to complete development immediately, have a definite plan, for it will in the long run save money and produce the unified effect that makes for maximum enjoyment.

One of the loveliest pools I know is shown on pages 106–107. Both the pool and the surrounding area were the creations of Thomas Church, the great San Francisco landscape architect. Except for its glowing green color, the pool itself is not exceptional. It's just a simple circle. But it is tucked into a hillside between the house and surrounding woods in such a way that it looks like a woodland pond. And this effect is further enhanced by the large rock garden directly above the pool. This is packed with handsome shrubs and ferns and down the middle runs a boulder-filled stream carrying water from the filter back to the pool.

Ringing the pool is a deck of pink brick on which Mr. Church placed, here and there, a few huge rocks like those in the stream. They provide places for swimmers to sit, and help visually to link the pool with the rock garden and woods. But their greatest value is their sculptured look. They are suggestive of great sea animals which have come ashore to bask in the sun.

The largest part of the deck area is occupied by the poolhouse, a pleasant shingled structure with big glass doors on the water side. Directly in front, a canvas awning provides shade. Mr. Church is frank to admit that the awning was an afterthought and that he is not altogether happy with it; but when it was found that the trees did not give adequate relief from the sun, this was the easiest way out. And other than Mr. Church, who is perfectionist enough to say that it detracts greatly from the scene?

Of course there are not many swimming-pool owners who would want to copy the design of this particular pool and the surrounding area even if they could. What you do with the area around your own pool is an individualistic matter just as this was. But the pool does serve to illustrate what can be achieved first by analyzing how the pool area is to be used and how it should look and then by drawing plans, one after another, until the goal is gained.

Fencing the Pool Area
I am rather skeptical of the value of a barrier around a swimming pool, because to some children it is a challenge rather than a deterrent. But in this age of permissiveness, when efforts to train children have been deferred, it is impossible for me to buck spreading legal insistence that every new pool must be surrounded with an unclimbable barrier at least 4 ft. high to keep children from drowning.

Like it or not, when you check your building code, you will probably discover that your new pool must be fenced. This is unfortunate, because there are few fences, walls or other barriers which add to the beauty of the swimming-pool area; and there are many which restrict its use. It is for these reasons that the fencing of your pool should be given attention before you proceed with the development of other parts and features of the surrounding area.

Your first objective should be to place the fence (I use the word loosely to include all other types of barrier) as far as possible from the pool. Ideally, if your lot is of average size, you should run the fence from the back wall of the house all the way around the boundaries of the backyard. Thus you give the yard unity and sweep which it would not have if you fitted the fence around the pool as a collar goes around a dog's neck. You gain privacy from your neighbors throughout the yard. You have ample room around the pool to relax and play to heart's content. And you not only make the fence less visible because it is farther away, you also acquire the space necessary to mass shrubs in front of it and thus hide it completely.

On the other hand, if there is good reason why you cannot fence the entire backyard, you should at least make sure that there is enough space between pool and fence so you won't feel confined. (The same rule applies if you own an exceptionally large lot or acreage which you would be silly to fence completely.) Like so many things about a pool-building project, how much space is enough space depends on the way you will use the pool area and on the design of the pool. For instance, if your children are over about nine years of age, they need more space than if they are under nine, because their activities and games are more wide-spreading. If you want to entertain huge gatherings at the poolside, you need more space than if your entertaining is limited to barbecuing steaks for six bosom friends. If you build a naturalistic pool, you will need more space than if you build a formal pool,

This pool by Thomas Church was dictated by the site; but the pool and its surroundings now make the site. Most people feel the pool and garden are informal, but Mr. Church considers it pretty formal. His theory is that it is not necessary for the pool to be informal, but that the people in the composition feel *informal*.

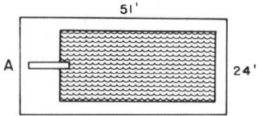

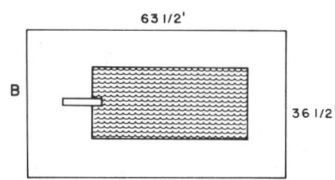

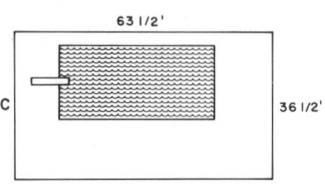

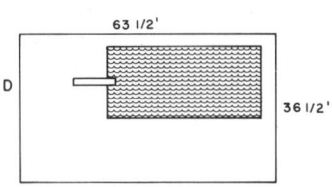

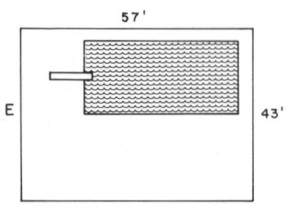

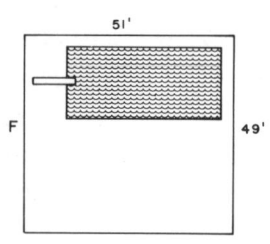

Six ways to fence an 18- by 38-ft. pool.

because you will have to surround it with more planting to enhance the natural effect.

Admittedly, the more space you allow between pool and fence, the longer the fence must be and the more it will cost. And even under the best of circumstances, an unclimbable 4-ft. fence is not cheap. In the Sears catalog, prices for 200 ft. of fencing range from approximately $265 for the cheapest grade of chain-link fence to $600 for the fanciest board fence. Shipping and installation costs are not included. But there simply is no escaping the fact that a major part of the fun of owning a pool is derived, not from swimming, but from lounging, sunning, playing, eating, etc., around the pool. That kind of fun is dependent on having elbow room.

Is it possible to attain this without spending a fortune on the fence?

Well, suppose you put in an 18-by-38-ft. rectangular pool with a 10-ft. diving board. At the very minimum, this requires a 3-ft.-wide walk around the two long sides and the shallow end and a 10-ft. space for the diving board at the deep end. Total area covered: 24 by 51 ft., or 1,224 sq. ft.

If you install a fence tight to these dimensions as in Sketch A, you need only 150 ft. of fencing and thus cut the bill from Sears about 25 per cent. But you will hate the installation with a passion because you have no freedom of movement. And psychologically, you will be even more restricted. If the fence is solid, you will feel as if you were in prison. If it's chain-link or the equivalent, you will be in a cage.

Now suppose you buy 200 ft. of fencing and add an equal amount—12½ ft.—to all four sides of the pool, as in Sketch B. The total area covered jumps to 36½ by 63½ ft. This gives you a little more than 9 ft. of space around the two long sides and the shallow end; and little more than 16 ft. at the deep end. More important, the square footage of the area has almost doubled to 2,318 sq. ft. Deducting the space occupied by the pool, actual ground area within the fence vaults from 540 to 1,634 sq. ft. You have gained all this for an additional cost of roughly $65–$150!

Despite the size of the ground area, however, its arrangement still leaves something to be desired, because there isn't too much you can do with the 9-ft. spaces around the sides and shallow end except to fill them with chairs and tables. So suppose you pull the fence in closer to the pool at one side and at either of the ends. Two possibilities are illustrated at Sketches C and D. Or suppose

108

you change the proportions of the fenced area but place the pool in a corner as in Sketches E and F. The ground area in all cases becomes more useful. The feeling of confinement you would have even in Sketch B evaporates, because even though the pool is hard up against the fence on two sides, there is ample space to stretch or to escape on the other two sides.

There are two obvious morals to be drawn from this let's-suppose exercise:

(1) A small increase in the length of a fence surrounding a swimming pool adds a disproportionately great amount of ground space. The table below gives an idea of what is to be gained if you increase the length of the fence around rectangular pools of different size by one-third. (For simplicity, I assume the pools have no diving board and the original fences—before they are increased in length—are placed within 3 ft. of all four sides of the pools.)

Pool size (ft.)	Total length of fence before increase (ft.)	Ground space around pool before increase (sq. ft.)	Total length of fence after increasing one-third (ft.)	Ground space around pool after increase (sq. ft.)
12 × 24	96	252	128	500
15 × 30	114	306	152	738
16 × 32	120	324	160	1024
16 × 36	128	348	171	1130
18 × 38	136	372	181	1241
20 × 40	144	396	192	1404
20 × 45	154	426	205	1596

(2) By off-setting the pool within the fenced area, you do not make any actual gain in ground space but you usually gain much more usable space. Under no circumstances, however, should a fence be placed less than 3 ft. from the side of a pool, because it would restrict safe passage around the pool. If plants are to be grown inside the fence to conceal it or to relieve its appearance, the fence must be pushed back so that the distance from the planting bed to the pool is at least 3 ft.

The type of fence you build (I continue to use the word loosely) is dictated partly by cost, partly by the fence's location, partly by surrounding buildings, and partly by the visual and functional effect you hope to achieve. Three of these factors need a little explanation.

If a fence is to be located where you—and hopefully your neighbors—cannot see it, or if it is to be hidden behind plants, use the cheapest, ugliest type available. (That is usually chain-link or other types of steel mesh.) But to use such a fence in a prominent location or even in a slightly offstage place where you cannot avoid seeing it is inexcusable. There is no reason under the sun why anyone should allow a swimming pool to wreck the appearance of a yard. On the contrary, a pool should be the basis for improving the appearance of a yard.

The buildings on your property should influence your selection of a fence primarily if the pool is close to them; but even if it is not, it is good to consider the materials of which the buildings are built so that there will be harmony between buildings and landscape. All this means is that if your house is, say, brick, building a wall of brick around the pool helps to tie the property together aesthetically. Similarly, if the pool is distant from the house and you have a big poolhouse of, say, simple flat plywood panels, building a fence of vertical rough boards will unify it with the poolhouse and simultaneously complement the poolhouse. Note, however, that while it is desirable to have your pool fence and buildings in harmony, it is not mandatory. Sometimes contrast is better. And sometimes—just to relieve monotony—it is a good idea to build a fence of two or three materials.

The functional effect of a fence is not always limited to keeping children out of the pool. You may want it also to increase your own privacy around the pool, to give your neighbors privacy from the pool (never forget that a pool can wreck neighborhood relations just as easily as it can cement them), or to ward off wind. Some fences, obviously, can do these things better than others.

What types of fence are available?

Chain-link is running away with the market because it is less expensive than anything else. It is easy to install, durable, takes up minimum space and keeps children away from a pool until they discover that if they take off their shoes, it's a lot of fun to climb. Be that as it may, the building authorities approve it wholeheartedly; so if your main aim is to keep them pacified, this is the easiest way.

The principal deficiencies of chain-link fencing are the following: By itself it has no value as a privacy barrier. It is completely ineffectual as a windbreak (it does, however, do a better job of catching leaves blowing across the yard than a solid fence, because the wind hits it head-on instead of vaulting over the top). It is a chore to paint. And it is an eyesore unless you conceal it. Green paint helps but is not the answer. You must either mass shrubs in front of it or bury it under vines.

I prefer shrubs because, if you don't plant them in a straight line, you soften the outline of the fenced area and give it a more informal, less restrictive feeling. On the other hand, if you plant them in a straight line directly at the base of the fence, they can be trained up on both sides to form a fine hedge with a steel center which can't be climbed because it is too hard to reach. In both cases, however, the shrubs add materially to the cost of the fence and eliminate its space-saving advantage.

If vines are used, they should be evergreen because, unlike shrubs, deciduous species are rarely so thickly branched that they can conceal the steel in winter. The best species are those which, like wintercreeper, send branches out to the sides as well as upward because they give "body" to the fence—obliterate its thin, harsh lines. But these, too, take up space. However, since they spread farther and faster than shrubs, they save you money because you need fewer of them.

Ornamental iron fences pretty much belong to the past, although you can have them made to order and can perhaps find them in a junkyard. They're also expensive; and because any unit over 4 ft. tall is likely to be very ornamental and imposing, they are suited only to formal pool settings. This is too bad, because they are excellent in most other respects (except as privacy barriers and windbreaks).

Brick walls are nearly perfect. They are so beautiful that you should make a feature of them. The natural color is soft (unless you make the mistake of using those ghastly yellow or brown bricks); they take paint well; the texture is interesting; they're exceedingly durable; and they occupy no more than 8–12 in. of ground space. Furthermore, they are impossible to climb, completely stop the view in or out and protect the area directly in their lee from wind. But the cost—!

Stone walls are in the same category. If anything, they are more beautiful. But they are normally somewhat thicker and cost even more.

Concrete block walls are considerably cheaper than both brick

111

and stone. I don't think they are very good-looking if laid up with staggered joints, as in a basement; but if a more decorative bond (joint pattern) is used or if smaller-size or textured blocks are used, the walls can be handsome. They should be painted, however.

Block walls are strong and thin (8 in.). They give complete privacy and protection from winds in their immediate lee. And most walls are unclimbable, but those made of ornamental pierced blocks are a cinch.

More or less solid wood fences are the ideal compromise between chain-link and masonry. The cost is reasonable even when the fences are made—as they must be—of redwood, cypress, red cedar or a wood impregnated with preservative, and are fastened together with nonrusting galvanized or aluminum nails. Installation is easy. Once up, you can let them weather to an attractive gray or stain them almost any color you like. They take up very little space. And they do not appear so forbidding as masonry walls if you build them higher than 4 ft. in order to gain greater privacy and to protect more of the pool area from winds.

But wood fences must be designed with care if they are to accomplish everything you want. To begin with, they must be built with vertical boards or timbers on the outside if they are to turn back climbers. This usually means that the inside surface facing the pool is an unsightly network of framing timbers. To conceal these, you must either nail up additional boards or plant shrubs.

If you want the fence to be a first-rate wind screen, the boards must be spaced 1 in. or more apart so that the wind will go through the fence and come out on the other side as a gentle zephyr rather

An attractive pool-area fence made of vertical boards spaced several inches apart on both sides of the timbers forming the frame. The fence is difficult to climb and a good privacy barrier. It is also an outstanding windbreak, since the wind hits it head on and is broken up as it filters through the open joints.

than sailing over the fence and coming down, force unabated, within a few feet of the lee side.

If all these requirements are to be met, choice of fence design is limited to a louvered fence and overlapping board fence. In the former, the vertical boards are set at about a 45° angle between the top and bottom rails. In the latter, wide boards spaced 2–3 in. apart are nailed vertical to both sides of the fence and the boards are staggered so you cannot see through the joints. The louvered fence is a better wind screen; the overlapping board fence a better privacy screen. There isn't much difference between them otherwise.

Fences made of plywood, asbestos-cement or reinforced fiberglass panels have much to recommend them, although they are not widely used. The panels are commonly 2 ft. wide and 6–8 ft. high. They are fitted into a framework of 2-by-4's so they look the same both front and back. They are as durable as wood, as easy to build, cost about the same or possibly a little less because they use less

A high fence of translucent plastic panels is an effective barrier to youngsters trying to invade a pool area and serves as an exceptionally attractive background for plants. You can even enjoy the tracery of the planting on the other side.

The author's pool. Because the false cypress hedge on two sides was not kept pruned before I bought the property, it crowds so close to the pool (even after hard cutting back) that it is actually difficult to get by it; and it contributes far too much debris to the pool. But I shall never cut it down, because it is an outstanding privacy barrier and wind-break, and a formidable barrier to trespassers. There is ample space for sitting and playing on the other sides of the pool.

material, occupy the same space and are just as hard to climb. They give privacy, but they are not very good wind screens.

Whether a hedge is as acceptable around your swimming pool as a fence or wall is a question you must answer by checking your local building code. In some communities it will pass muster; in others, it will not.

Actually, a hedge of stout shrubs—preferably with thorns or needles—will turn back children far faster than any fence. It is just as attractive as a fence or even more so. If allowed to grow high enough, it affords complete privacy on both sides. As a wind screen and leaf-catcher it is far superior to any barrier built by man. And it has the unique advantage of reducing the transmission of noise from one side to the other.

But a hedge has disadvantages, too. For one thing, if the law says you have to create an instant barrier, you must start out with large plants which cost quite a lot of money. It must be planted far

114

Handsome hemlock hedges and massed shrubs completely conceal the ugly, high chain-link fence which surrounds this pool area.

enough back from all sides of the pool so that its own falling and drifting leaves, twigs, flowers, etc., will not clutter the pool. (It must also be far enough back so that those wicked thorns will not wound swimmers.) And it must be trimmed regularly—at least on the pool side.

Removable Fencing Very few pool owners use fencing that can be placed close around the pool when it is not in use and removed during swimming hours. The idea has merit, however, because it reduces the amount of fencing required and at the same time permits you to have a spacious pool area when the fence is open.

In the most practical arrangement, a permanent fence or wall is built around three sides of the pool; the removable section is at one end separating the pool from the main deck area. This is usually made of chain link in wide sections which can be swung open on hinges or pushed back on large casters.

115

Gates   Like the fence, the gate in it must be unclimbable and at least 4 ft. high. It should have a self-closing and self-latching mechanism installed above a child's reach.

The Pool Deck   Although shrubs, groundcovers, ferns, etc. are often planted right up to the sides of naturalistic pools, most pools are completely surrounded by a paved deck. This serves several purposes: (1) It provides solid, nonskid footing for swimmers and bystanders. (2) It helps to keep grass clippings, soil and other debris out of the pool because it acts as a barrier between the pool and planting areas, is easily swept or vacuumed and, like a doormat, removes dirt from wet feet. (3) It keeps water splashed out of the pool from returning to the pool. (4) It may help to protect planting in the pool area from the splashed-out water.

As has been pointed out in several places, the minimum width of a deck is 3 ft. This is enough to provide safe passage around the pool; that, however, is all it does. Greater width is required wherever the deck is obstructed, as by a diving board or ladder, and wherever you plan to place your furniture; and it is desirable wherever the deck abuts a grass area—the principal source of the debris that gets into pools.

In other words, a pool deck is rarely of uniform width. It bulges out here, slims down there. But its outline usually conforms in a general way to the outline of the pool. That is to say, if the pool is round, the deck is round, although the two circles may not have the same center. Similarly, if the pool is kidney-shaped, the deck repeats the outer arc of the pool although it may not be completely kidney-shaped itself. Thus the deck emphasizes the shape of the pool rather than competing with it. (The design principle is the same as that followed in setting a precious stone in a ring or brooch.)

To keep pool water from draining back into the pool after it has been splashed out and to prevent storm water from running into the pool, the deck should slope away from the coping on all sides. A drop of 1 in. in 8 ft. is usually adequate. Actually, to get rid of pool water before it reaches the grass or other plants around the deck, some pool designers surround the deck with a narrow drainage ditch filled with gravel and covered with loose-laid bricks. It is doubtful, however, whether the small amount of water splashed from a pool contains enough chemicals to injure plants. On the other hand, if your pool is on a hillside, a drainage ditch between the deck and the uphill slope is needed to catch and divert storm water rushing down toward the pool. Alternatively, you might put in a catch basin with a grillwork cover. In either case an underground drain line should be installed to carry the water away from the area.

The material with which a deck is paved must be skidproof but not abrasive enough to feel uncomfortable or scrape the skin badly. It should be of a moderately light color—not white, which would blind you when you looked at it, or black, which would soak up heat and burn your feet. It must be durable and easy to clean. And it must, of course, be attractive and should blend with the fence or wall around the area although it need not be of the same material.

No material is perfect.

Ordinary concrete is excellent in all respects except one: It isn't pretty; and it doesn't get any prettier when you color it, or score it to resemble flagstones, or roughen the surface with swirly strokes of a broom, or press a pattern in it with tin cans, leaves or what-have-you. Nevertheless, very handsome concrete paving is easy and inexpensive to achieve.

One attractive type has a keystone finish which resembles travertine rock. This is made by dashing a soupy mixture of colored concrete on to an ordinary concrete slab, and then leveling it with a mason's trowel to form a surface which is smooth in some areas, coarse and pockmarked with small holes in other areas.

Another handsome concrete is coarse-aggregate concrete. This is made by pressing small pebbles or stone chips into ordinary concrete and then brushing and hosing the mortar away from around them so that they stand out slightly in relief. The resulting paving has a delightful texture which provides excellent footing without being too abrasive. The color depends on the pebbles used. You can have a pepper-and-salt combination by using pebbles of a single color in white concrete; or you can have a tapestrylike blend of several colors. The beauty of the paving may be further enhanced by laying it out in large squares separated by wide expansion joints or redwood strips.

The only real problem with either of these textured concretes is that they are difficult to sweep. Vacuuming is much better, especially on the keystone finish.

Brick makes a superb paving just as it makes superb walls. I admit it presents problems: It is easily stained by oil and other materials. In freezing weather, the bricks sometimes spall. The concrete mortar joints occasionally need to be remade. And in damp, shady locations, the bricks acquire a skin of moss which is extremely slippery.

But a well-made brick deck is durable, skidproof, easy enough to clean—and it is beautiful. I shall always be especially partial to soft pink bricks in the normal 4-by-8-in. size. But there are numerous good colors; and in recent years, there have been a number of new shapes which don't resemble bricks at all. Take a look at them, by all means. In addition to variations in color and shape, you should also remember that bricks can be laid in a great many interesting patterns.

Flagstone is another of my favorite deck materials. It is stronger than brick, stains a little less readily, and is about on a par with it for sweepability. The handsomest paving is made with cut squares and/or rectangles fitted neatly together to form an informal geometric pattern. This is particularly suitable to pools of geometric shape. But I find nothing attractive, as a rule, about flagstone paving which is made with irregular broken stones. The effect suggests a sheet of safety glass which has been hit with a sledgehammer.

In pool decks both flagstones and bricks should be laid in mortar. When laid without mortar on a bed of sand, they are prettier; but swimmers would stub their toes in the joints and sweeping is difficult.

(Incidentally, if you can find slate which is as rough as flagstone and is not too dark in color, it is excellent for decks, also.)

Quarry tile is a shade too slippery when wet to be an ideal decking material; but it is gorgeous stuff. Because it's available in myriad colors, shapes and sizes, there is virtually no limit to the designs you can create with it. And once it is down on a concrete base, it is durable, smooth and cool; washes spotlessly clean with the swish of a mop.

Kooldeck is a patented concrete which is especially popular in the Southwest because it is exceptionally cool underfoot. Laid in large, unbroken sheets, like ordinary concrete, it has a texture suggesting coral rock; is made in several pastel colors.

Although wood boards are very often used for decks around above-ground pools, their use immediately alongside in-ground pools is limited. But back from the pool edge they come into their own as an inexpensive means of providing a change of elevation in a flat pool area. They are also used to build terraces on a hillside above the pool.

Wood is not indestructible, of course. And it is often splintery. (The West Coast cedars are the best woods for decking because of their general freedom from splintering and resistance to warping; but because they are rather scarce, redwood is usually used.) Finally, wood needs occasional finishing with a penetrating stain if the silvery-gray of naturally weathered wood does not suit your decorative scheme.

On the other hand, wood is resilient under foot and always an ideal temperature. It is easy on the eyes even on the sunniest day. And it blends in with plants better than any other material.

Artificial grass will undoubtedly gain popularity as time goes by. The type made of nylon and resembling a golf green (this is the kind used on football fields) is pleasant to walk on even when laid—as it should be—on a concrete or asphalt base. If you have children, it provides better protection against abrasions and falls than other materials. And it is reasonably durable, resistant to chemicals and sunlight and easily vacuumed or washed with a hose.

The main objection to the material is its unnatural color and slipperiness whether wet or dry.

Indoor-outdoor carpet is used on decks but the only excuse I can see for it is that it is cheap and does a good, comfortable cover-up job on a badly laid or disintegrated masonry deck. It certainly is not suitable for a beautiful new pool installation.

Brick is one of the handsomest and all-around best materials for a pool deck. The coping is made of concrete but is not of bull-nose design.

Planting Around the Pool

No matter how sterile—strictly-for-swimming—your pool may be, it forms a lovely background—or perhaps I should say, foreground —for plants. Pools and plants go together, that's all there is to it; and if you want the area around your pool to be a truly inviting, relaxing, happy place to live many summer hours, you will surely put in quite a few plants.

Unless you are creating a naturalistic pool or going in for a bit of showmanship, all the plants should be well back from the pool edges. The most logical location for them is in front of and behind the fence and clustered around the poolhouse or around the filter and heater if these are exposed. The reason for this is that, despite their many charms, plants are responsible for a good part of the debris that falls into pools. The amount they contribute varies with the season, of course, and also with the peculiarities of certain plants (needled evergreens, for instance, shed their needles in warm weather). But I have never known a time of year when they were not shedding such things as leaves, twigs, insects, etc. Trees and large shrubs overhanging pools drop all this stuff directly into the water. But plants just a few feet back from the pool are little better. We have around two sides of our pool an old hedge of Sawara false cypress which at some time before we bought the place was allowed to go unpruned for several years. Consequently, even though I cut it back as hard as possible, the branches still extend to within 3 ft. or less of the pool and the dead needles that drop from it are forever blowing or washing into the water.

Another reason for keeping plants back from the edges of the pool bothers others more than it does me. It is the fear that treated water from the pool will damage or even kill the plants. Since I have referred to this problem before, I obviously do not pooh-pooh it, though I have never actually run into it. But this is not to say that plants have not been ruined by pool water, so there is no sense in taking chances and exposing yours.

One remaining reason for providing space—a minimum of 3 ft. —between pool and plants is that you need it to walk around the pool. Children especially need it as they chase around the pool so they can complete their journeys safely and so they won't batter the plants to bits in the process.

Plants nearest the pool should be planted slightly above the pool deck so that the soil around the roots and the water you apply will not spill out on the deck. Putting the plants in tubs and other big containers is an excellent idea because it allows you to change your planting scheme whenever you wish. If the plants are in the ground, build a curb around the bed 4–6 in. high; then fill in with soil, but keep it at least 2 in. below the top of the edging.

Away from the pool, you can plant at deck level, in a raised bed or in containers. If at deck level, try not to let the soil build up much higher than the deck so it drains out. Keeping a trench cut around the bed is a simple way to hold the soil in place.

There is no limit to the types of plants you can put in, although you should avoid flowers (except where planted in containers). The reason: they need fairly frequent cultivation, and that inevitably means that the soil around them spills out over the deck and gives you just one more clean-up problem. Trees, shrubs, groundcovers, ferns don't need cultivation.

Although you have many types of plant to choose from, you should be rather picky about the varieties you use. The best are those which are classified as "clean" plants: They do not shed twigs, branches, bark, fruits, seeds indiscriminately; they do not shed their leaves except in the fall about the time you are closing the pool.

On the reverse side of the coin, several kinds of plants you should avoid include:

Those with thorns (except in hedges around the pool area).

Those which attract stinging insects in vast numbers.

Those that drop fruits which stain paving (some plums are terrible offenders in this respect).

Some Selected Trees for the Pool Area

Species	Deciduous or Evergreen	Climate	Comments
Apple	D	Cold, temp., warm	Use late-ripening varieties
Ash, green	D	Cold, temp.	Very fast-growing
Beech, American	D	Cold, temp.	
Beech, European	D	Temp., warm	Plant well back from pool

Some Selected Trees for the Pool Area (Cont.)

Species	Deciduous or Evergreen	Climate	Comments
Birch, European	D	Cold, temp., warm	
Birch, white	D	Cold, temp.	
Camellia	E	Warm, warmest	
Cedar, deodar	E	Warm, warmest	
Cork tree, Amur	D	Cold, temp., warm	Needs lots of space
Crape myrtle	D	Warm, warmest	
Dogwood, flowering	D	Temp., warm	
Dogwood, Japanese	D	Temp., warm	
Fig, weeping	E	Warmest	
Franklinia	D	Temp., warm	
Fringetree	D	Temp., warm	
Ginkgo	D	Temp., warm	Plant male tree only
Grapefruit	E	Warmest	
Gum, lemon-scented	E	Warmest	
Hemlock, Canada	E	Cold, temp.	
Holly, American	E	Temp., warm	Prickly
Holly, English	E	Temp., warm	Prickly
Honeylocust, thornless	D	Temp.	
Jacaranda	D	Warmest	
Larch, Japanese	D	Temp.	
Linden, littleleaf	D	Cold, temp., warm	
Linden, silver	D	Temp., warm	
Magnolia, southern	E	Warm, warmest	
Magnolia, star	D	Temp.	
Mango	E	Warmest	
Maple, Amur	D	Cold, temp., warm	
Maple, Japanese	D	Temp., warm	Superb small tree
Maple, sugar	D	Cold, temp.	
Mountain ash, European	D	Cold, temp.	
Norfolk Island pine	E	Warmest	
Olive	E	Warmest	
Orange	E	Warmest	
Palm, royal	E	Warmest	
Palm, Mexican fan	E	Warmest	

Some Selected Trees for the Pool Area (Cont.)

Species	Deciduous or Evergreen	Climate	Comments
Peach	D	Temp, warm	Use late-ripening varieties
Persimmon, Oriental	D	Warm, warmest	
Pine, Austrian	E	Cold, temp.	
Pine, eastern white	E	Cold, temp.	
Pine, longleaf	E	Warm	
Pine, Scotch	E	Cold, temp.	
Poinciana, royal	D	Warmest	
Red cedar, eastern	E	Cold, temp.	
Schefflera	E	Warmest	
Seagrape	E	Warmest	
Snowbell, Japanese	D	Temp., warm	
Sorrel tree	D	Temp., warm	
Sour gum	D	Temp., warm	
Spruce, Norway	E	Cold, temp.	
Spruce, Serbian	E	Temp.	Needs less space than preceding
Sweet gum	D	Temp., warm	
Stewartia, Japanese	D	Temp., warm	
Tulip tree	D	Temp., warm	
Umbrella pine	E	Temp., warm	
Yellow-wood	D	Cold, temp., warm	
Yew, Irish	E	Warm, warmest	

Some Selected Shrubs for the Pool Area

Species	Deciduous or Evergreen	Climate	Comments
Andromeda, Japanese	E	Temp., warm	
Andromeda, mountain	E	Temp., warm	
Aucuba, Japanese	E	Temp., warm, warmest	Plant male and female specimens for berries

Some Selected Shrubs for the Pool Area (Cont.)

Species	Deciduous or Evergreen	Climate	Comments
Azalea	D or E	Temp. warm, warmest	Innumerable species to choose from
Bamboo, yellow-groove	E	Temp., warm, warmest	Silhouette against a wall
Beautybush	D	Temp., warm	
Blueberry, highbush	D	Temp.	
Box, common	E	Temp., warm	
Butterflybush	D	Temp., warm	
Camellia, sasanqua	E	Warm, warmest	
Cinquefoil, shrubby	D	Cold, temp., warm	
Cotoneaster, spreading	D	Temp., warm	
Cotoneaster, willowleaf	D	Temp., warm	Evergreen in warm climates
Elaeagnus, autumn	D	Cold, temp.	
Enkianthus, redvein	D	Temp., warm	
Euonymus, evergreen	E	Warm	
Euonymus, winged	D	Cold, temp.	
Fatshedera	E	Warm, warmest	
Fatsia	E	Warm, warmest	
Hawthorn, yeddo	E	Warm, warmest	
Heavenly bamboo	E	Warm, warmest	Silhouette against a wall
Hibiscus, Chinese	E	Warmest	
Holly, Chinese	E	Warm, warmest	Prickly
Holly, Japanese	E	Temp., warm, warmest	
Laurel, mountain	E	Temp.	
Leucothoe, drooping	E	Temp., warm	
Lilac, common	D	Cold, temp.	
Lilac, littleleaf	D	Temp.	
Lilac, Persian	D	Temp.	
Mahonia, leatherleaf	E	Warm, warmest	Prickly
Oleander	E	Warm, warmest	All parts of plant poisonous to eat

124

Some Selected Shrubs for the Pool Area (Cont.)

Species	Deciduous or Evergreen	Climate	Comments
Oregon grape	E	Temp., warm, warmest	Prickly
Osmanthus, holly	E	Temp., warm, warmest	Prickly
Peony, tree	D	Temp., warm, warmest	
Pine, mugo	E	Cold, temp., warm	
Pittosporum, Japanese	E	Warm, warmest	
Rhododendron	D or E	Temp., warm	Many species to choose from
Rose of Sharon	D	Temp., warm	
Skimmia, Reeves	E	Temp., warm	
Tamarisk, Kashgar	D	Temp., warm	
Viburnum	D or E	Temp., warm, warmest	Numerous species to choose from
Yew, Japanese	E	Temp., warm warmest	Plant parts poisonous to eat
Yew pine	E	Warm, warmest	

Some Selected Tall Hedge Plants

Species	Deciduous or Evergreen	Climate	Comments
Arborvitae, American	E	Cold., temp., warm	
Beech, European	D	Temp., warm	Needs much training
Box, common	E	Temp., warm	Makes a very wide hedge

Some Selected Tall Hedge Plants (Cont.)

Species	Deciduous or Evergreen	Climate	Comments
Cherry, Nanking	D	Cold, temp., warm	
Hemlock, Canada	E	Cold, temp.	
Elaeagnus, thorny	E	Warm, warmest	Wicked thorns
Hibiscus, Chinese	E	Warmest	
Holly, American	E	Temp., warm	Prickly
Holly, Chinese	E	Warm, warmest	Prickly
Holly, Japanese	E	Temp., warm, warmest	Plant tall, upright varieties
Honeysuckle, tatarian	D	Cold, temp., warm	
Myrtle, true	E	Warm, warmest	
Natal plum	E	warmest	Wicked thorns
Osmanthus, holly	E	Temp., warm, warmest	Prickly
Privet, Japanese	E	Warm, warmest	
Rose, shrub	D	Cold, temp., warm	Numerous species to choose from. All are thorny
Russian olive	D	Cold, temp., warm	Wicked thorns. Needs much space
Tallhedge	D	Cold, temp.	
Tea tree, Australian	E	Warmest	
Yews, Hicks	E	Temp., warm, warmest	Plant parts poisonous to eat
Yew pine	E	Warm, warmest	

13 Poolhouses

The extent to which Americans have changed their thinking about swimming pools is illustrated by what has happened to the little building near a pool. Once known as a bathhouse, it is now a poolhouse.

The change comes in part as a result of constant efforts being made by advertising and marketing men to "improve the image" of everyday things simply by changing the name. But there is no question that what used to be a utilitarian building for changing into and out of bathing suits has become a minor sort of home away from home.

What Do You Want a Poolhouse For? Obviously you don't need a poolhouse if your pool is directly outside your house. Neither do you need a poolhouse if the pool is far removed from the house. A poolhouse is not a necessity even though not having one means that swimmers must walk to the main house to dress or go to the bathroom. A poolhouse is a luxury pure and simple. But it is such a useful luxury that it is not hard to justify if you use it for well-thought-out purposes.

What are these?

Changing clothes.

Bathroom facilities—perhaps only a toilet and lavatory. But you should really have a shower so people can get clean before entering the pool. (If this is required at public pools, why not at residential pools?) Some people also like to shower after swimming.

Drying bathing suits and towels. This is likely to be part of the dressing room–bathroom area but may be a separate room. A small electric or gas clothes dryer is an asset.

Protecting the pump, filter and heater. This is not essential but it does prolong the life of the units somewhat. (Note, however, that if the poolhouse is a long way from the pool, the pump, filter and heater should be located somewhere closer to the pool in order to reduce the cost of the installation.)

Storing pool chemicals, pool equipment, furniture, toys, etc. This may require considerable space; then again it may not. In any case, the chemicals—especially the chlorine—must be stored in a dry room separate from the mechanical equipment.

Sitting in the shade. With all the American emphasis on sunbathing we tend to forget that it is a risky practice if overdone.

127

A modern version of a classical pavilion gives protection against the sun. Dressing rooms and storage space are in the structure to the right. The outlook from the pavilion is illustrated on page 33 (PHOTO BY JOHN D. ECCLES)

Shade near the pool is essential and one of the best ways to provide it is to extend the roof of a poolhouse out over the pool deck or simply to make the poolhouse a sun-shelter or, if you prefer, a pavilion with a roof and no sides.

Relaxing, entertaining, playing games, etc. Although in some elaborate poolhouses the area (or areas) provided for group activities is very specialized, it is usually nothing more than a sort of catch-all room, like the family room in the main house. The size of the room is flexible, but in view of the fact that the room is used almost exclusively in warm weather, it need not be large. By installing floor-to-ceiling sliding glass doors in one wall, you can open the room completely to the adjoining pool deck. Thus you have one huge indoor-outdoor room at very little expense.

Cooking. In most families, all the cooking in the pool area is done over an outdoor grill. But some families require a small kitchen including a refrigerator, range or oven, sink, perhaps a dishwasher, and certainly cabinets for storage of dishes, utensils, foodstuffs, etc.

Two circular, connecting dressing rooms are built of kiln-dried, clear all-heart redwood planks allowed to weather naturally. An open-air shower stall (foreground) partially screens the entrance. (PHOTO BY JEREMIAH O. BRAGSTAD FOR THE CALIFORNIA REDWOOD ASSOCIATION)

Almost hidden by lovely trees, shrubs and vines, this poolhouse serves also as a guest house.

Putting up overnight guests. Even since living in California years ago, I have been an enthusiastic backer of the guest house because it is an ideal way to take care of visitors. But who needs a guest house if they have a poolhouse? All you have to do is add a bedroom to the poolhouse and you're ready for anyone who comes along.

Design and Plan

Since a poolhouse is a specialized building—and so far in the history of the construction industry, a rather rare type of building—there is no source you can turn to for inexpensive, ready-made plans. In short, the plan and design for your poolhouse must be developed by (1) you, (2) a builder, (3) an architect or (4) a landscape architect. Of the four choices, I prefer the third if your poolhouse is large and reasonably elaborate, because an architect is trained to carry out unusual design assignments. I have little faith in builders as designers—even of conventional buildings—but they can be an enormous help if you want to work out your own plans.

How to go about developing a poolhouse plan is beyond the scope of this book. Planning any buildings is trickier than it looks. But the job can be done if you keep drawing *rough* plans, one after the other after the other, until you come up with a workable arrangement of rooms and spaces. Then, and only then, should you start to develop a plan which shows everything in precise scale and locates windows, doors, sinks, lavatories, pool filters, etc., exactly where they are to go.

Having done all this, you can start on the elevations of the poolhouse. Here is where a good builder can help, because, while he may not be a design genius, he should at least know how to arrive at a facade, side and back walls and roof that will look good. But don't trust him completely, at least until you make it clear how the poolhouse should look.

Here again you have many choices. But simply in the interest of giving unity to your property, you would be well advised to imitate the style of your house.

Stray Thoughts about Poolhouse Construction

Building codes. The placement of the poolhouse must, of course, comply with your building code. If it doesn't you must apply for a variance; and in my experience, town building authorities are loath to give variances on buildings which are not essential.

Also before seeking a building permit, you must make sure your code will even allow a poolhouse of the type you plan. For example,

Poolhouse of New England saltbox design incorporates a large living-eating-cooking room with a brick fireplace; and behind that, dressing rooms, a full bathroom and storage space. The huge door opening facing the kidney-shaped pool can be closed with screen doors in the evening; left wide open during the day when mosquitoes are less of a problem. In winter, plywood panels are slipped into the door frames behind the screen mesh. The small building at left— the owner calls it his corn-crib—houses the pool heater.

some communities do not permit anyone to build on a small-to-average-size lot a second building which might be used as a rental property. This means that a poolhouse with a kitchen, bathroom and entertaining room would probably be turned down.

Sliding glass doors. Be absolutely certain that these are made with safety glass. There is likely to be too much cavorting around in the pool area to put in anything else. If the doors have narrow frames or none at all, you should also paint some kind of design on each door—and on each section of fixed glass alongside—so that people will not walk into them.

Heating the poolhouse. Fireplaces are not noted for being efficient heat sources; but despite this, the best heating unit for a poolhouse is a fireplace because it gives off such a cheerful illusion of warmth. Its roaring or flickering flames mirrored in the pool act as a magnet in drawing people to the pool area; and once they are there, the color, aroma and sound of a wood fire cast a romantic spell over all.

Actually, if you want a fireplace not only for glamour but also for warmth, you can have one. Steel shells which funnel the heat of the fire into the room through ducts placed to the side of the fireplace have been available for years. When set on a concrete base and surrounded with brick or stone, they are indistinguishable from a conventional fireplace.

Small prefabricated metal fireplaces which are nothing more than sleek designs of the old Franklin stove are also fairly efficient heating units. They are particularly adapted from a styling standpoint to poolhouses of modern design.

In a large poolhouse, if additional heating is required, install small space-heaters in the exterior walls of each room. Use the same fuel source that is used for the swimming-pool heater.

Relief from the sun. Extending the poolhouse roof out over the deck is the easiest and most logical way to provide a shady sitting place around the pool. Since protection against rain is also desirable if you want to use the poolhouse for entertaining, the roof should be of solid, water-tight construction. For a simple poolhouse built mainly for functional purposes, however, you can erect a louvered or slatted roof. This gives less protection than a solid roof but should cost less.

Protection of another sort from the sun is provided by facing the poolhouse to the east or north so that people occupying it do not look into the glare of the setting sun.

*Sun-shelter and poolhouse create a complete living area far removed from the main house of a Sierra retreat. The structure, made of construction grade redwood for a natural look and low maintenance, houses dressing rooms, bar, sauna and equipment. Rocks along far side of the pool give it a semi-natural look. (*PHOTO BY JOSHUA FREIWALD FOR THE CALIFORNIA REDWOOD ASSOCIATION*)*

Storage. In addition to providing a dark, dry, locked storage space for swimming-pool chemicals, you also need storage throughout the summer for hand skimmers, brushes, brooms, the pool vacuum cleaner, toys, floats, extra poolside furniture, etc. Most of these things can be stowed away in a large closet (preferably opening outward rather than inward) in the poolhouse. But the average skimmer, pool brush and pool vacuum cleaner have handles that are too long for indoor storage. About the only way you can take care of them is to hang them on brackets or hooks on the back wall of the poolhouse or on a concealed part of the fence around the pool area.

Additional storage space for furniture, etc., that is taken in over winter is generally available in the dressing rooms and other parts of the poolhouse. If you have permanent built-in benches around the swimming pool, these may also be used for winter as well as summer storage if you build the bases like chests of waterproof masonry and cover them with solid, hinged lids.

14 Pool Enclosures and Indoor Pools

You build a pool; enjoy it for about four months of the year; and suddenly it comes over you, "My gracious! Here I've spent all that money for only four months of swimming. Now if I put in a pool heater . . ."

So you put in a heater; extend the swimming season a few weeks; and suddenly it comes over you, "My gracious! Here I've spent all that money for only five or six months of swimming. Why don't I enclose the pool and enjoy it year 'round?"

That's how swimming pools go under cover. More and more of them every year. I'm willing to bet that covered pools will never outnumber open-air pools. But their appeal is powerful. Very powerful.

Screened Pools The simplest kind of enclosed pool is surrounded on the sides and top with insect-screen mesh. It isn't commonly thought of as an enclosed pool because it is not designed to prolong the swimming season but simply to make life around the pool bearable in semitropical regions where mosquitoes go on the rampage in the summer and the sun is blistering. But it deserves at least passing attention.

Although some of the pool enclosures discussed further on may be equipped with screens in summer, the great majority of screened pool enclosures are homemade structures with straight sides 8–12 ft. high and flat tops. They are constructed of widely spaced, 2-in.-thick timbers with screen wire attached securely all the way around to keep out members of the nasty Culicidae family. Seen from outside, the enclosures look like cages. But inside, they are often planted to create delightful bowers made cool not only by the lush foliage but also by the screen mesh, which reduces incoming sunlight about 25 percent.

Air Bubbles The simplest and least expensive way to enclose a pool for use later in the fall and even all the way through the winter is to cover it with what most people call a plastic air bubble. Technically known as an "air-supported structure," this is defined by the Canvas Products Association International as "any building constructed of high strength fabric or film (or any combination thereof) which achieves its structural shape, stability and support by pretensioning with internal air pressure."

In its basic form, an air-bubble pool enclosure resembles a loaf of bread with the top half cut off and placed over the pool. Made of translucent vinyl fabric (often with transparent sidewalls), it is a huge bubble which is anchored around the sides to the pool deck and held open above the pool by air piped in from an automatic electric or gasoline-driven blower which operates continuously. Ingress and egress are through a small, tight-fitting door in one end of the bubble.

The pool in this bubble enclosure is used every day during the winter, even when temperatures fall below zero. Both pool and enclosure are heated, of course.

Although they may strike you at first as Rube Goldberg devices, air-bubble enclosures have withstood the test of time. They can be set in place and inflated to full size within about an hour. They will not collapse unless the blower stops operation for about thirty minutes or the fabric is ripped asunder. Loss of air through opening of the door or through small leaks has little effect. Because of their shape, smooth skin and stored-up warmth inside, the enclosures usually shrug off heavy snow. And because they are held down not only with ropes but also with large water sleeves, they are unaffected by high winds.

135

Unfortunately, like all other types of cold-weather pool enclosures, air bubbles by themselves will not permit year-round swimming or anything close to it. True, they admit and store up quite a lot of heat from the sun. But this is sufficient to extend the swimming season only four to six weeks into the fall. It has almost no effect on the start of swimming in the spring, because pool water takes almost as long to warm up under a bubble as in the open. In other words, if you were trying to decide which would do you more good—an air bubble *or* a pool heater—you would have a difficult choice, because they both add roughly the same number of days to the swimming season.

The real way to get maximum value and pleasure out of an air bubble—or any other cold-water pool enclosure—is to equip the installation with heaters that allow you to swim in comfort the whole year 'round. More about these heaters further on.

As opposed to other pool enclosures, air bubbles can be put up, taken down and stored with little effort; so they are rarely left standing during the summer. They should last three to five years before succumbing to the ravages of the sun. They cost from 75 cents to $1 per square foot of deck and pool area covered.

The bubbles are available in sizes to cover all normal residential pools. All ready-made units have a rectangular ground plan; but special shapes can be produced to order. Although their maximum height equals half their width, they must be several feet wider and longer than a pool in order to provide adequate headroom above the deck at one end and along one side. For example, a 20-by-40-ft. rectangular pool should be covered by a bubble with inside dimensions of about 24 by 45–50 ft.

Simple Framed Pool Enclosures

In a framed enclosure, the plastic, fiberglass or glass roof and walls are laid over an aluminum framework. (In a do-it-yourself enclosure, the framework is made of wood.) The resulting structure is more rigid than an air bubble and is less likely to collapse; but because it must be bolted to the deck to keep it from being carried skyward by winds, it is usually kept standing the year 'round.

The simplest kind of framed enclosure is shaped like a Quonset hut. It is made with semicircular ribs spaced 4 ft. apart and held together with longitudinal braces. Because the ribs are perpendicular to the length of the pool, headroom along the sides of the pool is

Pool enclosures of this type have a permanent aluminum framework covered with flexible plastic film. To hold down the size and cost of the enclosures, they are usually placed close to one side and one end of the pool, as in these two examples. Deck space for moving around and sitting is thus limited to the opposite side and end. The height of the structure is equal to half its width.
(PHOTOS BY
LORD & BURNHAM)

limited unless you install an enclosure which is at least 4 ft. wider than the pool. The end walls, however, are straight up and down.

The enclosures are completely swathed with several types of translucent or clear material. Polyethylene film is the cheapest; but while it is not seriously affected by cold weather, it breaks down under sunlight and must be replaced annually at a cost of $100 or more.

Vinyl fabric is considerably more durable; but unlike polyethylene, it does not transmit ultraviolet rays so you can get a tan in

137

the enclosure. If left in place on the framework, the fabric will last three to four years; but since this would make an enclosure unbearably hot in the summer, the fabric on the ends is usually removed to allow air to sweep through. Handling reduces the life of this material. Saran screening may be installed in its place.

Translucent corrugated fiberglass panels constitute the most durable covering for simple pool enclosures. They have a life expectancy of twenty years and because of their strength, they give the entire enclosure extra rigidity and load-bearing capacity. But they do not permit you to get a tan.

The panels may be used to cover the entire roof of an enclosure but are more often used only near the peak. The lower portions of the roof and the end walls are covered with vinyl which is removed in whole or in part for summer comfort. As in an all-vinyl-covered pool enclosure, Saran screening may be installed in place of the material that is taken down.

Per square foot of deck area covered, a polyethylene enclosure costs approximately $1.90; a vinyl enclosure, $2.60; and a fiberglass enclosure, $3.25.

The largest simple framed enclosure listed by the company which produces most of them is 32 by 72 ft.; but there is nothing to prevent adding more sections to stretch the length.

Elaborate Framed Enclosures

These are greenhouses pure and simple. Frequently they incorporate special arrangements which permit them to be opened wide to let in summer breezes; but in the final analysis, they are the same buildings that are used for raising plants.

They have peaked roofs; high, straight sides and end walls; are glazed with glass or reinforced fiberglass. Since they are pretty expensive to start with, there is no sense in putting up an enclosure which is only slightly larger than the pool. These are luxury units designed to give you complete freedom in and around your pool. As a consequence, one manufacturer offers seven standard widths ranging from 22 to 50 ft. and six standard lengths ranging from 24 to 66 ft.

Heating a Pool Enclosure

To maintain water and air temperatures in a swimming-pool enclosure at comfortable levels during the winter, you need one heater for the water and another for the air. (So-called combination heaters are made; but they really consist of two separate systems within the same shell.)

138

This type of pool enclosure is essentially a greenhouse but is designed so it can be opened wide for ventilation on warm days and in summer. Here the roof panels at the ridge slide down over the lower panels. Roof and walls are made of fiberglass. (PHOTO BY SUN/FUN POOL ENCLOSURES)

An ordinary swimming-pool heater is usually used to heat the water. The size suitable for summer heating is equally good for winter heating. Air is heated by any one of the methods used to heat air in greenhouses. You can install hot-water radiators around the sides of the enclosure, or you can install an air heater with a powerful blower at one end of the enclosure close up under the roof. The size of the heater can be figured reasonably closely from information given to customers by Lord & Burnham.

From the table below, jot down the heat-load factor for your size of enclosure. Multiply this by the air temperature you'd like to maintain in the enclosure minus the lowest outside temperature at which you expect to use the pool. The result is the total heat requirement in Btu's per hour for the enclosure. The heater you install should have a heating input at least equal to this requirement.

Example: You plan to install a 22-by-48-ft. pool enclosure. You want an inside air temperature of 80°. You expect to swim on days as cold as minus 5°. To calculate the Btu heating requirement of the enclosure, multiply 2,255 (the heat-load factor) by 85 (indoor temperature minus outdoor temperature). The answer is 191,675 Btu's.

Lord & Burnham Heating Table

Enclosure size (ft.)	Heat-load factor
22 × 36	1,790
22 × 40	1,945
22 × 44	2,100
22 × 48	2,255
27 × 48	2,905
27 × 52	3,100
27 × 56	3,295
27 × 60	3,490
27 × 64	3,685
27 × 68	3,880
32 × 52	3,805
32 × 56	4,035
32 × 60	4,265
32 × 64	4,495
32 × 68	4,725

Indoor Pools The basic difference between an indoor pool and a pool in an enclosure is that it is surrounded (but not necessarily completely surrounded) by solid walls and a roof rather than by glass or plastic. Because of this, much less heat is gained from the sun; and the loss of heat to the outdoors is much more gradual. This makes for—or should make for—more even, easier-to-maintain air and water temperatures in the pool area. On the other hand, because of the tightness of the construction and greater insulating value of the wall and roof materials, the humidity in the pool area is often so high that it causes discomfort to people and does serious damage to the building materials.

For example, one of my neighbors some years ago had one of the country's leading independent pool contractors put in a small indoor exercise pool. The pool installation was perfect; but the builder evidently knew little about engineering and construction of pool rooms, because within a year the plaster walls and ceiling had been so weakened by the high humidity that they had to be torn out and replaced with ceramic tile.

This gives some idea of the difficulties of building a successful indoor pool. You cannot trust just a pool builder—even an expert—to do the job. You should also employ a professional heating and ventilating engineer—preferably one who has already had experience with indoor pools—to advise not only on the heating and ventilating of the enclosure but also on its construction.

Generally, in an indoor pool the water and air are heated separately, the water being a few degrees cooler than the air. Air heating is done by baseboard radiators along the walls supplemented by warm-air inlets over the pool. In order to hold the relative humidity to a desirable 50 per cent, dry outdoor air is introduced more or less continuously into the pool room and heated. As it is circulated through the room, it absorbs the water vapor given off by the pool and is then exhausted outdoors. Condensation on the walls and windows is prevented by keeping the dew point of the room air below the inside surface temperatures of the walls and windows.

The first step in the metamorphosis of a swimming pool. Here it is a large, handsome outdoor pool surrounded by beautiful planting, deck and terraces. But the owners decided they would rather have a pool they could use the year 'round.

So they added to the house a large L-shaped wing incorporating an entertaining room with a tiny kitchen, a bathroom and a huge pool room. This picture, taken from about the same angle as that preceding, shows the end of the pool room.

Instead of building a completely new pool, the owners, in effect, cut the old pool in two. The shallow end (in the first picture, it is the right end) was kept as a small outdoor pool. It is shown here under its winter cover, which needs to be pumped dry and tightened.

The central sloping section of the old pool was filled in; and the deep end was lengthened and enclosed in an enormous room surrounded on three sides by sliding glass doors. The high ceiling is paneled in dark wood. The deck is made of concrete with a keystone finish. The pool is finished in black plaster.

Another view of the indoor pool. The door at right leads to the new entertaining room. The large windows look out on the old terrace, and behind that, the main part of the house.

When he decided he wanted an indoor pool as well as an outdoor pool, the owner of this property scouted around and found an old greenhouse which he erected on field-stone foundations two floors below the main floor of his house. From the house, the pool room is entered by a circular stairway. A smaller greenhouse at the end of the pool room (pictured at far right) is used for growing plants. Partly to save heat and partly to obscure the view of the pool from outside, translucent fiberglass panels were installed above the greenhouse glass (with an air space between) some time after the pool was built.

The ideal way of controlling conditions in indoor pools has not been found, however. New ideas are constantly coming along. Recently, for example, it was found in several large public indoor pools that if the pool water was not heated, it got up to within four degrees of the air temperature and held at that point; and for some reason, relative humidity within the pool room did not go higher than a rather dry 45 per cent.

Or consider the experience of one of my friends, a large manufacturer of heating equipment. He hankered to build an indoor pool for three years, but because he's not a fellow to do things carelessly or by halves, he resisted all temptations to get going until he had consulted with just about every authority he could find. The pool installation he eventually made at very considerable expense is not only beautiful but also works. Nevertheless, after a year's happy

144

swimming, he was not altogether happy with the elaborate ventilating system which had been installed; and in an experimental mood one day he shut if off and plugged in an ordinary little electric dehumidifier of the type used to keep basements dry. It now does a better job of controlling humidity in the pool room than the special system—and at lower cost.

Other important problems which must be coped with in an indoor pool are noise and light.

To keep the pool room from reverberating with noise until you begin to think the roof will fly off, the ceilings and walls should be covered with moisture-resistant acoustical materials. Large glass areas should be covered with fiberglass or other moisture-resistant draperies. For maximum sound control, the deck should be covered with indoor-outdoor carpet; however, this is such drab, soggy stuff that if you pick something a little less efficient—travertine concrete, for example—no one can blame you.

Underwater lighting in an indoor pool is essential for safety. The wattage of the light, or lights, should figure out to 1 per square foot of pool surface. (This is more than an outdoor pool requires.)

Overhead lighting in the pool area should be sufficient to allow you to see clearly where you are going; but the very high light levels called for in public pools are unnecessary. The fixtures should be located where you can relamp them easily, without turning into a gymnast. Hanging a light directly over the pool is just asking for trouble.

15 Swimming-Pool Chemicals

If you have strong feelings about the use of chemicals in this modern world, don't build a swimming pool. Without chemicals you simply cannot run a pool safely. You must use them not only to purify the water so it cannot cause infection whether you drink it or absorb it through your skin but also to clarify it so that you can see through it without the slightest effort.

Disinfectants These are the pool owner's first defense against the disease- and infection-producing organisms that may abound in a swimming pool, and also against algae and other undesirable elements. Chlorine in one of its several forms is the chemical upon which greatest reliance is placed. For one thing, it was the first used in general water treatment. More important, it is effective, widely available, reasonably inexpensive, easy to use, has good staying power (or, if you prefer a more technical term, builds up a residual), is compatible with other pool chemicals and is not harmful to health, skin or eyes if properly used.

In residential pools, chlorine is most often used in the following forms:

Calcium hypochlorite is available as a granular powder and in tablet form. Containing 70 per cent available chlorine, it is a potent enemy of bacteria and algae if the pH* of your pool is between 7.2 and 7.6; and it is economical to use. But it leaves a residue which clouds the water and may not wash out of a sand filter as well as it should.

The easiest way to use granulated calcium hypochlorite is to walk around the pool and scatter it by hand over the water. Tablets can also be scattered but are best placed in the skimmer. I have heard it said time and again that a much better way to use the powder is to dissolve it in a crock of water before introducing it to the pool, because this settles out the residue; but don't believe it. To dissolve the powder completely, you need a much larger crock than you can possibly handle.

Calcium hypochlorite must be used in sufficient concentrations to maintain in a pool at all times a free chlorine residual of 0.6–1.0 parts per million (or ppm). For initial treatment of a pool, use the material at the rate of 1 oz. per 1,000 gal. of water. Thereafter,

* The technical terms used in this chapter are fully explained in Chapter 16.

147

you should use 3–4 oz. per 5,000 gal. per day. For super-chlorination treatment, use 1 oz. per 500 or 1,000 gal. of water, depending on the problem to be solved.

Because calcium hypochlorite is highly combustible, it must be stored in a dry, clean, tightly covered container in a cool, dry place. Never mix it directly with any other chemical or material; nor carry it from its container to the pool in a dirty receptacle; nor handle it in any way with tools or equipment dirtied with other materials. And never handle it while smoking. If fire should break out, drench it and the area surrounding with water. If the chemical spills, douse it well with water and flush it away.

Calcium hypochlorite which has been treated to make it less flammable is produced by several firms; but even it must be handled with care.

Sodium hypochlorite is nothing more than household liquid bleach with 10–15 per cent chlorine. It is sold generally in opaque plastic containers which must be kept in a cool, dark place and used quickly to prevent loss of strength. Frequently, it comes mixed with caustic soda to make it last longer; but because this raises the pH of the pool water, occasional treatment with acid is necessary to lower the pH to the desired 7.2–7.6 range.

Unlike calcium hypochlorite, sodium hypochlorite does not leave a residue, but it may cause deposits in equipment which is used to feed it into the pool if the water it is mixed with is hard. Pouring straight from the bottle into the pool avoids this problem. The amount of sodium hypochlorite to apply in a pool depends on the strength of the chemical. The aim, however, is to maintain a free chlorine residual of 0.6–1.0 ppm.

Lithium hypochlorite, a fairly new form of chlorine, is a granular material with 35 per cent available chlorine. It is stable in storage; dissolves completely and rapidly when scattered over the pool; is an excellent bactericide and is usually an excellent algicide. But after a heavy rain or spell of hot, bright weather, the dosage must be increased briefly to keep algae under control.

In the first treatment of a pool, lithium hypochlorite is applied at the rate of 3–4 oz. per 1,000 gal. of water. Thereafter, to maintain the recommended free chlorine residual of 0.8 ppm, add 4 oz. per day to each 8,000 gal.

Chlorinated iso-cyanurates are concentrated organic chemicals (as opposed to the above inorganic materials) which disinfect pool water and simultaneously protect the chlorine from destruction by the sun. Used only in a stabilized pool (see below), they are long-lasting (residuals do not dissipate quickly) and need not be added to the pool so often as hypochlorites. Furthermore, they leave no residue.

One form of iso-cyanurate is a granular material designated NaDCC which is usually used only every other day. Another form (TCC or TCCA) is a tablet or stick which is usually introduced through an automatic chlorinator but may be placed in the skimmer or a dispenser which floats around the pool. One 7½-oz. tablet can chlorinate 8,000 gal. of water for more than a week. In both cases, follow the manufacturer's recommendations for the exact amounts to be used. The general aim, however, should be to maintain 1.0–1.5 ppm of free chlorine residual in the pool at all times. The pH of the water can range from 7.2 to 7.8.

Bromine and iodine are also used for disinfecting swimming pools but to a very limited extent. The one advantage claimed for both is that they are less irritating to the eyes than chlorine. Iodine is exceptionally stable and its effectiveness is not appreciably changed by the pH of the water. On the other hand, both materials cause problems which militate against their use.

Stabilizers Stabilizers—sometimes called conditioners—are used in newly filled pools to stabilize the chlorine and thus to retard the rate at which it is dissipated by sunlight. This treatment is particularly popular in warm climates where it is difficult to maintain a free chlorine residual in an unstabilized pool.

Cyanuric acid is the chemical now usually used. It is a non-toxic, granulated, white powder without disinfecting powers; but it reduces the amount of chlorine that is required for pool treatment throughout the summer.

For a pool to be properly stabilized, you should maintain a level of 30 ppm of cyanuric acid. This is attained by adding acid to the pool in the spring at the rate of about 2½ lb. per 10,000 gal. (You also need ⅓ lb. of soda ash for each pound of acid to keep the pH above 7.0.) If you then disinfect the pool with chlorinated iso-cyanurates, no additional cyanuric acid should be needed for the rest of the year; but if you use a hypochlorite as disinfectant, small amounts of cyanuric acid must be added periodically.

Whichever type of chlorine is used to disinfect a stabilized pool, you should strive to maintain a free chlorine residual of 1.0–1.5 ppm. (Note that this is higher than the residual required in an unstabilized pool.)

Water-Chemistry Regulators

Muriatic acid and sodium bisulfate are acid chemicals used to lower the pH and total alkalinity of swimming-pool water. Muriatic acid is a corrosive liquid which must be handled with extreme care since it can cause serious burns. It can also etch concrete and metal. So when using it, wear rubber gloves and take care not to spill it. Another problem with muriatic acid is that it lowers the pH of pool water so abruptly that it is likely to cause a chemical imbalance in the water which, among other things, causes irritation of eyes.

Use acid of 32 per cent strength and add it directly to the water at the deep end of the pool. The table indicates how many fluid ounces are needed per 1,000 gal. of water to lower pH.

Lowering pH with Muriatic Acid

PRESENT pH	DESIRED pH		
	7.0	7.5	8.0
8.0	1.1 oz.	0.3 oz.	—
8.5	1.3	0.6	0.2 oz.
9.0	1.8	1.0	0.7
9.5	3.2	2.5	2.1
10.0	5.5	4.7	4.4

Sodium bisulfate, a dry, granular chemical, is safer to use than muriatic acid. And because it acts much more slowly, it has less tendency to etch the pool walls and floor and does not make the water uncomfortable to swim in.

To use sodium bisulfate, simply scatter it more or less evenly over the water at the deep end of the pool. Apply the chemical at the rate of 1 lb. per 5,000 gal. to lower pH one point.

Note that when lowering the pH of a pool, you should never add more than 1 lb. of sodium bisulfate or 1 pt. of muriatic acid per 5,000 gal. of water at one time.

Soda ash (sodium carbonate) is the principal chemical used to raise the pH of water. It comes in granular or tablet form, and is scattered over the water at the deep end of the pool. The table shows how many ounces (by weight) are required to treat 1,000 gal. of water.

Raising pH with Soda Ash

PRESENT pH	DESIRED pH		
	7.0	7.5	8.0
5.0	19 oz.	23 oz.	26 oz.
5.5	18	22	25
6.0	15	19	22
6.5	9	13	15
7.0	—	4	6

Sodium bicarbonate (baking soda) is used instead of soda ash when it is necessary to raise the total alkalinity of pool water with only a slight increase in pH.

Iron control is a liquid chemical which is added to pool water to prevent it from turning reddish-brown when it is chlorinated. The chemical is required only in water containing high concentrations of iron, manganese or copper. If you know before filling your pool that the water has enough iron (the main troublemaker) to discolor the water and cause staining of the pool finish, you should add the iron control when filling starts. No discoloration will follow. But if you don't know that the water contains iron, don't worry: adding the chemical after the discoloration occurs will correct matters in short order.

Apply iron control at the rate of 1 oz. per 1,000 gal. of water. One treatment lasts the entire season, although it is advisable to add small quantities every now and then when fresh make-up water is introduced from your water system. (Rainwater, however, is of no concern since it is free of impurities.)

(Another way to correct mineral-staining of pool water is to add extra chlorine and run the filter for 48 hours or more. Combined with the chlorine which discolored the water in the first place, the extra chlorine oxidizes the minerals remaining in the water so they can be removed by the filter.)

Alum, more properly called aluminum sulfate, is a flocculent—

a gelatinous chemical which surrounds and clings to particles in water, thus forming larger particles which are easily trapped as they pass through a filter. Its ultimate purpose is to improve the action of filters in removing turbidity from pool water.

Alum is a virtual necessity if you own an old pool with an old rapid sand filter. But it is rarely used with high-rate sand filters and is never used with DE or cartridge filters.

Alum is usually introduced into the circulating system after backwashing. The pH and alkalinity of the water must be high, because alum is acid and may upset conditions in the pool otherwise. The alum is placed in the skimmer and drawn into the filter from there. Occasionally, if a pool is exceptionally turbid, alum is scattered over the water surface and allowed to settle overnight. (The pump and filter should be shut down.) The accumulated dirt is then removed from the bottom the next morning by vacuuming.

Sequestering agents are chemicals which are used occasionally in sparing amounts to keep hair oils, suntan oils, body oils, etc., in solution and prevent them from forming scum rings around the sides of the pool. They are generally needed only in pools which are heavily used by teen-agers.

Algicides   Algae are microscopic aquatic plant growths which are present almost everywhere; develop and grow in the presence of light even in cold weather; and multiply extravagantly in hot, sunny weather. There are many species—mostly green in color but some black or brown. If you are a scientist, it may amuse you to figure out to which group a particular pest belongs; but to the average pool owner, one is the same as the other and all are bad.

Actually, algae are not harmful to people; they do not make a pool unusable. But they may turn water green and often make it so turbid that you can't see through it for more than a few inches. They attach themselves to pool walls and floors—particularly those which have any roughness—grow in clusters and spread into large mats. And they may not only leave stains on the walls and floors but also make the surfaces as slippery as a banana skin.

Normally, if you chlorinate a pool properly and maintain the recommended chlorine residual, algae are quiescent; and as long as you super-chlorinate the water periodically during the summer, they will usually stay that way. But every once in a while they get out of hand—or at least threaten to get out of hand. When that happens, you have a choice of either giving the pool such a massive dose of chlorine that it must be shut down for about a week or using an algicide. The latter treatment is preferable because it's easier, less expensive and does not interfere with the use of the pool.

Algicides are made of several different chemicals. Some of the compounds are algistatic, meaning that they prevent growth of algae; others are algicidal, meaning that they kill established algae; and still others are preventives as well as killers. If you depend on chlorination to control algae, use the algicidal or combination type if algae should start to grow. The alternative, if you don't rely on chlorine as a control, is to use an algistatic material on a regular basis (usually every three to four days) throughout the summer.

16 Treating the Pool Water

Treating pool water is a two-part operation. It involves (1) filtering the water and (2) keeping it properly conditioned with chemicals. When I am asked how much time the job takes, my usual offhand reaction is: "A lot." But if you were to press me for details, I'd have to admit that the treatment of water—apart from other chores around the pool—actually goes quite quickly. But it does demand attention.

Running the Filter In most residential pools the pump and filter are sized to give one complete turnover of the pool water every 12 hours (that is to say, all the water in the pool passes through the filter at least once during this period). This does not mean, however, that all pool owners run their filter exactly 12 hours a day. Some run them less; some, more.

In practice, filtering for less than 12 hours daily is recommended only when the water is rather cool and the pool gets relatively little use. But many pool experts and owners feel that 24-hours-a-day filtering, day in and day out, is highly desirable—much better than 12-hour filtering—because it keeps the water that much cleaner. Furthermore, 24-hour filtering is almost a necessity with DE filters, since the diatomaceous earth may fall off the filter elements whenever the filter is stopped and must be recoated before the filter is started up again. However, it is worth noting that 24-hour filtering runs up the electric bill rather substantially. In 1972, when I never turned off my filter except for backwashing, I spent $75 more for electricity than in 1971, when I ran the filter on a half-day schedule.

However you schedule your filter operation, there is not much work to be done. The only regular job involves cleaning.

On modern filters, the time for cleaning is indicated by one or two gauges mounted on the tank. (On my high-rate sand filter, for example, cleaning is called for when the difference in the pressure shown on the two gauges has decreased to 15 lb.) When the time arrives, stop the pump. Close the valve on the suction and return lines if the system is located below the surface of the pool. Clean out the leaf strainer in the pump; then replace the strainer and cover, and open the suction and return valves.

Now turn the large multiport valve on top of the filter from "filter" (normal operating position) to "backwash" and start the pump. Keep an eye on the waste water pouring from the backwash line. As soon as it runs crystal clear, stop the pump again, reset the control to "filter," start the pump and resume filtering of the pool water.

If your filter is of a type which is not cleaned by backwashing, follow the directions in the manufacturer's operating manual. After a DE filter is clean, you must either feed new diatomaceous earth into it or redeposit the old earth on the filter elements. In either case, the water flow through the filter should be throttled down slightly until enough dirt has built up on the filter elements to reduce the water flow to its designed rate.

Basic Facts about Chemical Treatment of Pools

The purpose of filtering swimming-pool water is to remove not only all particles that make the water cloudy but also those organic particles that indirectly increase the demand for chlorine by providing food for bacteria and algae. The purpose of treating pool water with chemicals, on the other hand, is not only to kill bacteria and algae but also to oxidize and thus destroy an assortment of elements, such as oils and minerals, which may change the color of the water or make it cloudy or smelly. Chlorine is the chemical most commonly relied on to achieve this goal. But if you were to treat your pool water with chlorine only, you would be sorely disappointed with the results. The reason is that chlorine can be fully effective only if the pH, alkali content and ammonia content of the water are in balance with it.

You might say, therefore, that the treatment of swimming pool water is a balancing act—and a rather tricky one, at that—until you have worked at it for several months.

The main aim is to maintain in the pool at all times a free chlorine residual of sufficient size and strength to destroy any bacteria and other undesirable matter which may enter the pool between chlorinating treatments. This means that every time you add chlorine to the pool, you must put in enough to control not only the contaminants which are in the pool at that very moment but also those which will be carried into the pool by wind, swimmers, etc., within the next 24–48 hours.

The amount of chlorine residual is expressed as so many parts of free chlorine per million parts of water. (Free means that the chlorine is in the form of pure hypochlorous acid, a potent disinfecting and oxidizing agent.) Parts per million is abbreviated "ppm."

By test and through experience, professional swimming-pool operators have concluded that in the average pool the actual size of the chlorine residual should range between 0.6 and 1 ppm. Below 0.6, the residual might not be enough to take care of bacteria and algae. Above 1.0, the chlorine might be irritating to a swimmer's eyes, ears, nose or throat.

Unfortunately, chlorine residuals are never completely stable, because several things are constantly striving to sap their strength. The sun, for instance, dissipates chlorine rapidly, especially on long, hot, dry summer days. High water temperature also dissipates chlorine. Similarly, chlorine is used up faster in a pool filled with swimmers than in one occupied by a single person.

These are problems over which the pool owner has little, if any, control. But other antiresidual elements are another matter. One of these is the pH of the pool water.

The symbol pH is used to measure the acidity or alkalinity—sometimes called basicity—of water. Water with a pH of 7.0 is said to be neutral. Above 7.0, it becomes increasingly alkaline, or base. Below 7.0, it becomes increasingly acid.

The direct effect that pH has on the quality of swimming-pool water becomes apparent when the pH drops below 7.0 or goes above 8.0. Below 7.0, the water is irritating to swimmers, may corrode metals and may damage other pool materials. Above 8.0, the water is likely to appear cloudy and to cause formation of scale in the pool plumbing system. Of even greater importance, the alkaline water sharply reduces the effectiveness of chlorine as a disinfecting and oxidizing agent; and the only way you can make up for this—but not completely—is to add a great deal more chlorine to the pool than is normally called for.

For these reasons, the pH of pool water must be corrected by the addition of soda ash if it is lower than 7.0 or by the addition of acid if it is higher than 8.0. The ideal range for which you should strive is 7.2–7.6. It is within this range that a free chlorine residual has maximum disinfecting power.

Total alkalinity is another problem which may have an adverse effect on the ability of chlorine to control bacteria and algae. Total alkalinity is defined as the total amount of alkaline chemicals found in pool water. The degree of total alkalinity—measured in parts per million—regulates the pH of water. For example, water with very low total alkalinity responds more radically to efforts to change pH than water with normal alkalinity. On the other hand, water with very high total alkalinity may show very little response to efforts to change pH.

Fortunately, the total alkalinity of pool water can be changed with the same chemicals which are used for changing pH. The total alkalinity range you should aim for is between 80 and 100 ppm. Within this range, it is a simple matter to maintain pH at 7.2–7.6.

The third problem you must contend with in your efforts to maintain an effective free chlorine residual is ammonia. This common chemical, a nitrogen derivative, enters pools in various ways but most notably via urine and skin excretions. Once present in a pool in a sizable amount, it draws hypochlorous acid to it as a magnet attracts steel. The resulting reaction produces compounds called chloramines; and what had been a free chlorine residual becomes a combined chlorine residual.

Since chloramines are not very effective as disinfecting and oxidizing agents and since they may cause eye irritation and give water an unpleasant chlorine odor, a combined chlorine residual is not desirable. You should therefore take steps either to rid your pool of ammonia or to tie up the hypochlorous acid so that it will not combine so readily with ammonia. The first step is accomplished by super-chlorinating the pool periodically; the second, by stabilizing the pool with cyanuric acid.

Testing Pool Water for Chlorine Residual and pH

The only way anyone can keep swimming-pool water in a balanced state so that chlorine can be effective is to keep the water tested. Testing is a simple, quick task but one which must be done carefully to assure accurate results and to permit accurate pool treatment without waste of expensive chemicals.

The most important tests are for pH and free chlorine residual. These should be made daily—and perhaps even twice a day—at the start of the swimming season and during the hottest summer months. Ideally, they should also be made daily throughout the period in which the pool is in use; but such frequency need not be maintained at times when the tests are producing uniform results day in and day out. Even in this pleasant situation, however, you must never forget that conditions within a pool can change radically without warning.

The same kit is used to make both tests. In its most popular form it consists of two dropper bottles containing chemical reagents and a hand-size piece of rigid, clear plastic with two open vials, or cylinders, to hold pool water. One vial is used to test for residual chlorine; the other, for pH. Adjacent to each vial is a series of very small cylinders each permanently filled with a liquid of different color and each marked with numbers indicating the results of the test.

The first step in using this test kit is to read the directions accompanying it. Follow these to the letter. If, for example, the directions call for adding five drops of one of the reagents to a water sample, add five drops—not four or six.

Between tests, keep the kit in its case or a box so it doesn't get dirty or pick up any sort of contaminant; and keep it out of the sun.

When making a test (this should be done just before you add chemicals to the pool), wash your hands or rinse them thoroughly in the pool. Swish the plastic vials through the pool water several times to make sure they are clean. Then reach down into the pool as far as possible (12–18 in. at least) and fill the vials with water. Generally, it is best to take the water from the deep end of the pool, though this is not mandatory. Just do not take it from in the vicinity of the inlets.

Remove the plastic container from the pool and pour water from the vials until they are filled to the "fill" lines marked on each vial. The water in each vial will have a slightly curved surface, known as a miniscus; the bottom of the miniscus in each vial should be exactly level with the fill line. This operation sounds like child's play, but is actually surprisingly difficult. You may have to fill and empty the vials repeatedly until they contain exactly the right amount of water. If you get discouraged, use a clean medicine dropper to fill the vials.

As soon as the water samples have been taken, the tests should be completed. The reagent which is most often used in the test for chlorine residual is a yellowish liquid named ortho-tolidine; that used in the pH test is a red liquid named phenol red. Add these in the specified amounts to the chlorine residual and pH vials respectively. Then cap the reagent bottles tightly.

Cover each vial with a cork or cap, never with your fingers, since body acids may give a false test reading. Hold the plastic container in one hand and shake it to mix the contents. Then hold the container against a bright, white surface—not up to the sky— and compare the colors of the water samples with the colors of the adjacent small cylinders.

The sample in the vial used for measuring pH will range from yellow through orange to purple-red. As the numbers adjacent to the small cylinders show, yellow indicates that the pool water has a pH below 7.0. Orange shading to red is in the 7.2–7.6 range. Red is in the 7.6–8.0 range. And purple-red indicates a pH of 8.0 and over.

The sample in the chlorine residual vial ranges from almost white, indicating a residual of only about 0.1 ppm, to deep yellow, indicating a residual of 1.0 ppm. In testing for chlorine residual, the color reading should be made no more than 15 seconds after the reagent is added to the water sample. The result tells you pretty closely how much of the chlorine residual is in the free state. If you then set the sample aside, out of the sun, for about five minutes and take a second reading, you may find that the color of the water has deepened. This increase in color indicates how much of the chlorine residual is available in the combined state. If the combined residual exceeds the free residual, this is an indication that you should do something to "burn out" the ammonia in the pool.

After completing the tests, rinse the plastic container—and especially the water vials—thoroughly. If you have any reason to believe that any of the ortho-tolidine reagent accidentally got into the vial for testing pH, soak the vials in a detergent solution and then in water for several hours before using them again; otherwise the ortho-tolidine, which is acid, will upset the pH reading in future tests.

Test kits of the type described cost anywhere from $3 to $9. Although they might seem like an extravagance, the more expensive kits eventually pay for themselves because the color samples are more accurate and therefore give more accurate readings; thus you may be able to save on the amount of chemical used in the pool. In all cases, when the bottles of reagent are used up, refills are available at a fraction of the total kit costs. But be sure to use the refills sold by the original manufacturer of your kit. Using Company A's reagents in Company B's kit is likely to produce erroneous test results.

Although the ortho-tolidine test for chlorine residual is the most popular, it is not always the most accurate. Because of this, several new test kits have been introduced in recent years. In one, known as the DPD test, the reagent is put up in tablet form and consists of a compound identified as diethyl-p-phenylene-diamine. The tablet turns the water sample to a pink or red color which gives you the reading for the free chlorine residual in the water. To find the total free and combined residual readings, additional tablets must be added to the sample.

The other new test method is called Aqua Check. This is a test for free chlorine residual only and for pH. The testing device is a small strip of rigid plastic with two round holes in one end. To use the device, hold it well below the surface of the pool and agitate it vigorously until bubbling from the hole in the very end of the strip stops. Then immediately compare the color of the material in the end hole with the purplish color samples printed on the container in which the strips are sold and stored. After half a minute, comparison of the color of the second hole with a second row of yellow and green color samples on the container indicates the pH of the water.

Aqua Check test is made by dipping the plastic strip into the pool and then checking the color in the two holes against the samples on the side of the container.

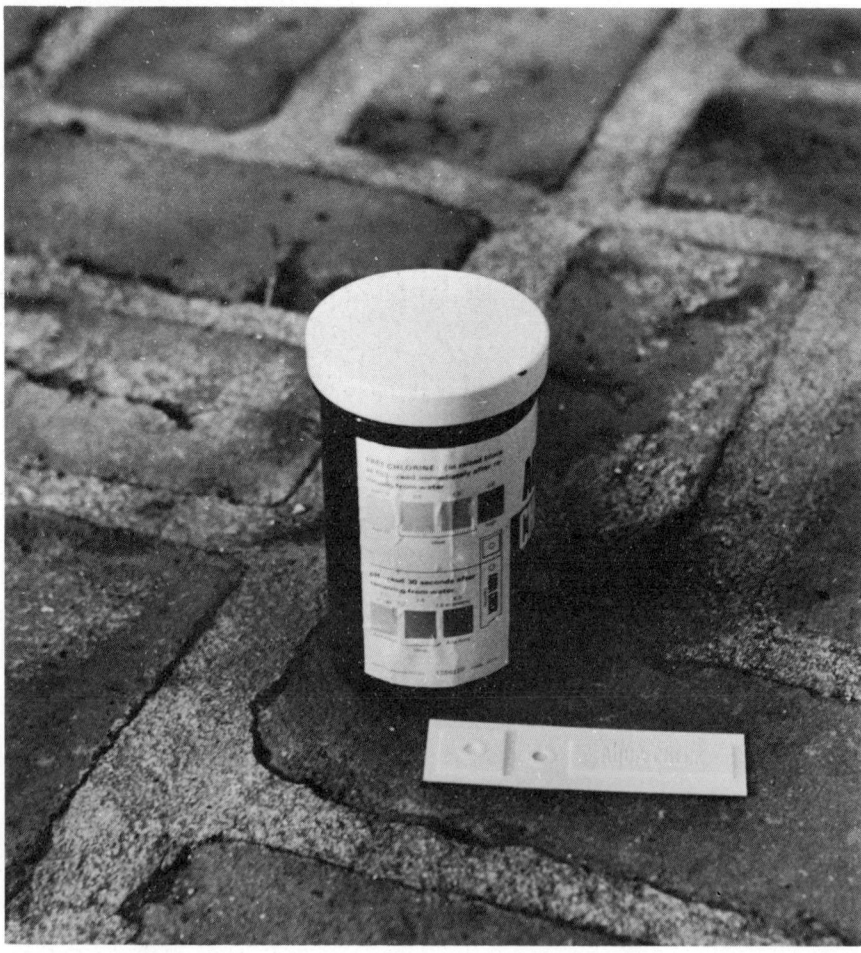

Testing Pool Water for Total Alkalinity

To test your pool for total alkalinity, you should buy either a small kit made specifically for the purpose as a supplement to your chlorine residual and pH test kit, or a large $12 kit used for all-purpose testing.

All-purpose test kit for testing chlorine residual, pH and total alkalinity.

To make a test, fill the vial to the indicated line and add one drop of each of two reagents. This turns the water violet. Then, counting each drop, add a third reagent until the water changes to a light yellow or white. Multiplying the number of drops of the third reagent by 10 tells you what the total alkalinity is in parts per million. (For example, ten drops equals 100 ppm.)

161

Planning How to Treat Your Pool

Three points should be settled before you start chemical treatment of a pool:

(1) How much water does the pool hold? This is an essential piece of information. Without it you cannot possibly know exactly how much chemical should be added to the pool to achieve the desired results.

If your pool has a more or less even slope from one end to the other—that is, if the shallow section, sloping intermediate section and deep section are of about equal length—the average depth is easy to determine simply by measuring the depths at the shallow-end wall and at the deep-end wall, totaling the figures and dividing by two. (The answer usually comes out to about 5½ ft.)

To figure the gallonage of a rectangular or almost rectangular pool, you then simply multiply the length of the pool times the width times the average depth times 7.5. (There are 7½ gal. in 1 cu. ft. of water.)

If the pool is round or very close to round, multiply the square of the radius times 3.14 times the average depth times 7.5. The alternative—not quite as accurate—is to measure the diameter times the diameter times the average depth times 5.9.

In an oval pool, measure the length times the width times the average depth times 5.9.

The volume of oddly shaped pools such as boomerangs, Y's and T's is figured, in effect, by cutting the pool into its principal pieces, calculating the volume of each piece, and then adding all the pieces together.

In the case of kidney-shaped, teardrop, naturalistic and other exotically shaped pools which are not readily divisible into pieces, draw the pool to scale on a piece of graph paper on which one square equals 1 sq. ft. Then total the number of squares and partial squares within the outline and multiply the answer by the average depth times 7.5.

The most difficult of all pools to figure are those in which the bottom does not have a more or less even slope or in which the bottom slopes not only from shallow end to deep end but also from each side toward the middle. Here the only solution is to divide the pool into areas—shallow, intermediate and deep—and to calculate the volume of each area as well as you can. To do this, you may find it helpful to draw a three-dimensional plan of each area. The alternative is to run water at full speed from the faucet you will use to fill your pool into a vessel of known size, such as an oil drum. Time how long it takes to fill the drum. Then by timing how long it takes to fill the pool to capacity, you can quickly calculate by proportion how many gallons the pool holds. (Example: If it takes exactly 3 minutes to fill a 50-gal. drum with water, and it takes 6,000 minutes to fill your pool, the pool holds approximately 10,000 gal.)

(2) Which type of chlorine will you use and what brand? Actually, this is not a crucial question. There is little difference between the pool chemicals turned out by different manufacturers. There isn't, in fact, very much difference in the ultimate effect of different chemicals of the same basic type. If you want to start with calcium hypochlorite as a disinfectant, then decide to change to sodium hypochlorite, and then change again to a chlorinated isocyanurate, you can do so.

Nevertheless, if you do switch from one type of chlorine to another, or if you stabilize a pool which has been unstabilized, you can expect some temporary problems with the water which will necessitate additional treatment (mainly for pH) to balance the water again. For this reason, since I often find chemistry baffling, I prefer not to make radical changes in the course of pool treatment during the swimming season. I'd rather muddle through the year with the old treatment course, making whatever minor changes are called for, and begin the next year on an entirely different course.

(3) At what time during the day will you treat your pool? Setting up and sticking to a definite schedule is helpful mainly because you get into the habit of doing what has to be done: you don't give the pool water a chance to play tricks just because you neglected to treat it when you should.

The best time to treat a pool is in the early evening or early morning. If you run your filter 24 hours a day, evening treatment is better because the water has plenty of time to assimilate the added chemicals before swimming starts the next day. But if you run your filter less than 24 hours a day, it's necessary to treat the pool in the morning, when you start the filter.

Starting Up a New Pool   Since it is the simpler operation, consider the filtering of the water first.

Although no harm will be done by starting the filter before the pool is filled, it is generally advisable to wait until filling has been completed. You should then set the multiport valve on the top of the filter to "drain." This is necessary to clear all the pipe lines of debris which may have got into them during the construction process. Prime the pump, turn it on and let the water coming through the filter drain out on the ground for several minutes until it is running full and clear. Then stop the pump.

If you have a sand filter, turn the multiport valve to "backwash" in order to settle and level the sand and remove any very fine particles. Turn on the pump once again and let it run for three minutes until the waste water runs clear. Then stop the pump, switch to "filter," start the pump and begin normal filtering operations.

If your filter is of the DE or cartridge type, start them at "drain" to clear the pipe lines. The cartridge filter is then ready for normal operation. The DE filter, however, must be given a "precoat" of diatomaceous earth. Follow the directions for the make you own.

Treatment of the water with chemicals can start before the pool is completely full, although this is not essential. The first step is to make a test for total alkalinity and pH. If the alkalinity test reveals a content of between 80 and 100 ppm alkali, your water can be considered perfect on this score at least. Even if the content is between 50 and 80 ppm, you are in luck: no treatment for alkali is needed. But if there are less than 50 or more than 100 ppm alkali, the water should be corrected.

If the total alkalinity is low, add sodium bicarbonate to the pool at the rate of 2 oz. per 1,000 gal. This should raise the alkalinity to the desired level without raising the pH too much. (If you used soda ash instead of sodium bicarbonate, it would raise the pH sharply but would have little effect on the alkalinity.)

On the other hand, if the total alkalinity is too high, you must add acid to bring it down. For fastest results, use muriatic acid. Sodium bisulfate is slower but safer. Use the amounts specified in Chapter 15.

Whether you are trying to raise or lower total alkalinity, you should bear two points in mind:

(1) Total alkalinity changes more gradually than pH; therefore it may take repeated treatments to bring it into the desired range. This is especially true when it is being reduced. One of the phenomena encountered in areas with very hard water is that, when acid is added to water, the alkalinity drops a little while the pH drops precipitously. Then within a short time the pH bounces right back up almost to its original reading.

(2) To give the alkali content time to respond to treatment, wait at least 12 hours before making another treatment. A second rule noted in Chapter 15 is that you should never add more than 1 pt. of muriatic acid or 1 lb. of sodium bisulfate per 5,000 gal. of water at any one time.

As soon as you have established the total alkalinity for your pool water, turn your attention to the pH problem. Actually, in the process of correcting total alkalinity, you may also have brought pH into the 7.2–7.6 range. If so, no further treatment is required. But if the pH is still high, continue adding sodium bisulfate or muriatic acid, but at a reduced rate. If the pH is still too low, add soda ash at the rate recommended in Chapter 15.

If you have a new concrete pool or a newly plastered pool, however, don't be surprised if it takes some time to make the pH settle down in the 7.2–7.6 range. In this kind of pool, alkalis "bleed" from the walls and floor for several weeks after filling; and until this stops, the pH shoots back up to an undesirably high level after every acid treatment.

Continuing Control of pH and Total Alkalinity

The initial balancing of total alkalinity and pH does not mean you can forget them for the rest of the summer. On the contrary, you should continue testing for pH every time you test for free chlorine residual; and changes should be made with acid or soda ash whenever readings drop below 7.2 or rise above 7.6. Be on the alert particularly for sudden rises in pH, since they are likely to indicate the presence of algae even though the pests are not to be seen.

Testing for total alkalinity need be done only once a month. If it is found to be rising—the normal situation—add acid to the water.

Controlling Hardness in Water

Hard water is a problem in all states except Maine, New Hampshire, Massachusetts, Rhode Island, Connecticut, Delaware, Maryland, Virginia, the Carolinas, Georgia, Alabama, Mississippi, Oregon and Washington. It is an especially serious problem in Indiana, Illinois, Iowa, the Dakotas, Nebraska, Kansas, New Mexico and Arizona.

Hard water not only feels unpleasant to the skin but, more important, it causes scale to deposit on pool walls and in the pool plumbing system (particularly in water heaters and automatic chlorinators).

Since hardness in pool water is caused in part by some of the chemicals that contribute to total alkalinity, the best way to control it—though not completely—is to maintain total alkalinity at 80–100 ppm. The principal causes of hardness, however, are calcium chloride and calcium sulfate and, to a lesser extent, magnesium chloride and magnesium sulfate; and since these do not respond to treatment for alkali content, they not only remain in the pool water but build up as the water is evaporated by the sun.

Short of running the water through a softener—a very expensive proposition—control of hardness attributable to calcium and magnesium is virtually impossible. Testing for it once a year indicates whether it is increasing greatly, but accomplishes nothing else. About the only thing you can do is to remove scale deposits as you see them by scrubbing with dilute muriatic acid. You should also empty the pool every three years and refill with fresh water.

Treating a Pool with Granular Calcium Hypochlorite

If you start up your pool in hot, sunny weather, chlorine should be introduced as soon as the pool contains several thousand gallons of water; and further treatments should be made until it is full. However, there is no point in testing the water during this period. Just add roughly 1 oz. of chlorine per 1,000 gal. of water, and trust that it will keep down any algae which try to become established.

If you are filling the pool in the spring, however, chlorination can wait until the pool is nearly full. But don't wait until you have balanced the total alkalinity and pH. True, your initial chlorine treatments probably won't be fully effective until the alkalinity and pH problems are solved; but the treatments should keep algae and bacteria within reasonable check.

For the first treatment of a filled pool, add 1 oz. (by weight)* of chlorine per 1,000 gal. of water. This ought to satisfy the immediate demand for chlorine (that is, it should be sufficient to kill the contaminants already in the pool) and produce a residual; but the only way you can be sure there is a residual is to test the water a couple of hours after treatment. If this shows less than 0.6 ppm of free chlorine, add 1¼ oz. of chlorine per 10,000 gal. at once.

Daily tests for chlorine residual should be made thereafter throughout the swimming season, although every-other-day testing is permissible in periods when the residual and pH show little fluctuation. The exact amount of chlorine required to maintain a residual of 0.6–1.0 ppm depends on the test results; but as a rule, addition of 3–4 oz. per 5,000 gal. every day will do the trick.

* 9 oz. of chlorine by weight equals one 8-oz. kitchen cup.

During hot, sunny weather and at times when the pool is getting heavy use, it is advisable to make weekly super-chlorination treatments to prevent build-up of algae and to rid the water of chloramines. Such treatments—which are a substitute for, not a supplement to normal daily treatments—consist of 1 oz. of chlorine per 1,000 gal. of water. Add the chlorine in the evening, and do not permit swimming until a test has been made the following morning to determine whether the residual, which may rise as high as 10.0 ppm, is back down to a safe level of 1.0 ppm or lower.

In the event that algae or objectionable odors develop in the pool despite periodic super-chlorinations, a super-super-chlorination treatment—often called a shock treatment—should be made promptly. Use 1 oz. per 500 gal. of water. Do not permit swimming until the chlorine residual has returned to 1.0 ppm or lower.

Note: The preceding directions apply only to granular calcium hypochlorite. Directions for use of tablets vary with the brand.

Chlorinating a Stabilized Pool

Stabilizing your pool is necessary if you disinfect it with a chlorinated iso-cyanurate. Stabilizing may also be done if you use calcium hypochlorite or any of its less well-known hypochlorite relatives. In either case, the purpose of stabilization is to increase the stability of the bacteria-killing hypochlorous acid in the pool water and so prevent its rapid dissipation by the sun.

Treatment of a pool which is to be stabilized starts with adjusting the total alkalinity and pH to the proper levels. This is followed by the addition of 1 oz. of calcium hypochlorite per 1,000 gal. of water. Let the filter run for 12 hours. Then add cyanuric acid and soda ash at the rate specified in Chapter 15 or as recommended by the manufacturer of the acid. Your goal is a concentration of 30.0 ppm or higher.

After continuing filter operation for another 12 hours, you should inaugurate routine chlorine treatments. If using an iso-cyanurate, follow the dosage recommendations of the manufacturer (there is too much variation between formulations to give specific directions here, although as a rough average you should use 1 oz. per 1,000 gal. per week). On the other hand, if you use calcium hypochlorite, add 2 oz. per 5,000 gal. every other day. In both cases, test for free chlorine residual (as well as for pH) daily. It should be maintained at 1.0–1.5 ppm.

To guard against algae infestations and to destroy chloramines, super-chlorinate the pool periodically with 1 oz. of calcium hypochlorite per 1,000 gal. of water. This treatment is required once a week during hot, sunny weather and/or when the pool is filled with swimmers; every other week, otherwise.

If algae do get a foothold or the water develops a strong odor, shock-treat the pool with 1 oz. of calcium hypochlorite per 500 gal. After shock treatment and super-chlorination, swimming should not be allowed until the chlorine residual subsides to 1.5 ppm or lower.

A final step which must be taken in the management of a stabilized pool is to check the cyanuric acid content every two to three weeks. This is done with a small test kit made specifically for the purpose. The acid level should be held at 30.0 ppm or higher.

If Rain Floods a Pool

Normal rainfall has little effect on swimming-pool treatment because it does not dilute the water enough to throw test readings far out of line. Violent storms are another matter, however, because they introduce too much water and also bring in algae and other undesirable elements which contribute to the loss of chlorine. It follows that you should test your pool carefully following heavy rains, and adjust the chemical treatment as necessary.

Hiring a Pool Service

I well recall that shortly after my wife and I bought our house and pool in eastern Connecticut, my brother and his wife bought a house and pool in the Los Angeles area. After several months of tedious effort to gain control of my pool, I asked my brother in a letter how he was getting along. "Just fine," he wrote back and let it go at that.

I confess to being slightly disappointed. Misery loves company. And then the truth came out. Ben wasn't taking care of his pool at all. He had hired a service.

Pool services have been in existence in California and Florida for a long time, and a great many pool owners employ them. A few of the services are sizable firms; but most are one-man outfits. Largely through experience supplemented sometimes by training received from big pool builders who don't want to be bothered with servicing, these men become pretty adept at cleaning, testing and generally maintaining pools and correcting problems which arise. But obviously they add substantially to the cost of owning a pool. And even if that is no deterrent to your employment of a service, be warned that you cannot find one in all communities.

On the other hand, if you're "lucky" (I put lucky in quotes because my brother's experience over a period of several years seems to indicate that pool services are not all pure gold), you should take the following steps when hiring a service:

(1) Check whether the laws of your state, community or town require pool services to be licensed; and if so, make sure the firm you hire has a license which is up-to-date.

(2) If the service employs servicemen, check whether it has workmen's compensation insurance covering them. It should also carry liability insurance to cover against injuries to you and others for which it may be responsible.

(3) Make sure the chemicals used by the service are known brands which are registered under federal and state laws. Never permit use of homemade concoctions.

(4) Enter into a signed agreement with the service—and be sure before you sign it that you understand it perfectly.

17 Opening an Old Pool in the Spring

Getting the pool ready for the swimming season is a job I always look forward to and relish even though it is sometimes a bit onerous. Most of all I like the prospect of lolling in and around the pool on the bright summer days that I know will soon come along. But secondarily, I enjoy working down inside the momentarily empty pool because even on late March days it is a protected pocket of sunlight and warmth.

Opening a Full Pool in Good Repair

Here are the steps to be taken:

(1) Remove the cover and ice buffers. Spread the cover out on the lawn to dry before folding it, or better, rolling it up and storing it.

(2) Remove leaves, sticks and other large debris from the pool bottom with a leaf skimmer, leaf rake, pool brush and/or a jet vacuum cleaner. This is a tedious job, especially if the water is very murky, but it is preferable to using the regular pool vacuum and risking clogging of the suction line.

(3) Remove the winterizing plugs in the pipe lines. Uncover the pump. Close the drains in the pump, filter and heater. Replace the gauges on the filter. Reinstall the automatic chlorinator.

(4) Brush down the pool walls and bottom.

(5) Prime the pump and start filtering the pool water on a 24-hour-a-day basis. Backwash the filter frequently.

(6) Replace ladders, diving board, slide, etc.

(7) As soon as the water is clear enough, inspect the walls and floors for stains and remove them.

(8) Test the water for total alkalinity and pH, and adjust as necessary. Test for cyanuric acid in a stabilized pool, and adjust.

(9) Test for chlorine residual and add chlorine as specified in Chapter 16.

Allow at least five days to get a pool back into condition for swimming after it has been closed down for a long time.

Opening a Pool If You Don't Save the Water

Some people, as a matter of course, empty and refill their pools with fresh water every spring. Although this is wasteful of water and chemicals, it satisfies some feeling of fastidiousness—and who is to say there is anything wrong with that? On the practical side, it also permits more thorough cleaning and inspection of the pool.

But emptying of a pool is not necessary to having sparkling pure water unless the water is very hard. In that case, a pool should be refilled every three years in order to prevent the build-up of scale in the plumbing system and on the pool walls.

Whatever your reason for emptying a pool, the process of getting it ready for the swimming season is similar to that outlined above. But before you begin the job, remember that if the water table is high, your pool may be pushed up out of the ground when it is empty or only partially empty if it does not have a hydrostatic relief valve; so if you have had unusually heavy precipitation during the winter or if local building contractors and pool builders are experiencing trouble with flooded excavations, you will be smart not to empty the pool at this time. On the other hand, if the pool has a relief valve or if you are reasonably sure the water table is normal, you can start to empty it at any time.

The first step is to remove as much of the large debris as possible with a leaf skimmer or rake or a jet vacuum cleaner in order to avoid possible clogging of the suction line and predictably frequent cleaning of the strainer in the pump. The alternative, if you happen to own a portable submersible pump, is to empty the pool with this instead of the pool pump. Since it does not become clogged by debris, you can pump the water down to within a few inches of the bottom and then quickly take out the debris in buckets.

Once the pool is empty, brush down the walls and floor, and scrub them clean with a solution of chlorine bleach. Rinse well. Then fill the pool.

Test and treat the water according to directions in Chapter 16. Reactivate the pump, filter and heater as above; and replace the equipment around the pool.

Repairing Cracks and Holes in an Empty Pool

If the pool is painted concrete, vinyl or fiberglass, follow the directions in Chapter 20.

If the pool is finished with white plaster, cracks are repaired by scraping them open and filling with white polysulfide rubber sealant or silicone rubber sealant. Big breaks in plaster, however, should be repaired by a qualified plastering contractor—preferably the one who plastered the pool in the first place. On the other hand, if the plaster has deteriorated so much that you decide to paint it, you can easily fill the cracks and holes yourself with latex cement.

171

Repairing Ceramic Tile

If tiles are loose or broken, remove them. Scrape off old adhesive from the wall underneath and from the backs of the tiles. Butter the tiles with silicone rubber sealant and stick them back in place. Allow the sealant to dry for 24 hours; then fill the joints with a grout made of one part white Portland cement and one part fine white sand.

Replacing Concrete or Terrazzo Bullnose Coping

If the concrete in which the coping stone was embedded is sound, the simplest way to reset the stone is to chip a little off the top of the concrete and clean the back of the stone. Dry both surfaces thoroughly. Then smear silicone rubber sealant on the concrete and press the coping stone into this. Fill the joints around the stone with concrete mortar.

If the concrete under the coping stone is badly eroded, chip it out entirely. Coat the top of the pool wall with a soupy grout of Portland cement and water. Immediately trowel a heavy mortar made of one part Portland cement and three parts sand over the grout and press the coping stone into this.

Repainting Over Sound Rubber-Base Paint

If you are not certain which type of paint is now on your pool, peel off a piece about 1 in. sq. and ask your paint dealer to send it to a manufacturer of swimming pool paints for analysis. It is very important that the new paint be compatible with the old.

On the other hand, if you know for certain that the pool is now covered with a rubber-base paint, use a chlorinated rubber paint to recoat it.

Remove loose, scaling and powdery paint with a putty knife, wire brush and/or coarse sandpaper. Fill cracks and holes in the concrete. Wash the walls and floor with oxygen bleach or trisodium phosphate, and rinse well. Wash again with a solution of one part 32 per cent muriatic acid and one part water; and rinse once more.

Let the pool dry thoroughly before painting. If it was full of water over winter, it must be allowed to dry for at least a week before chlorinated rubber paint is put on.

Apply one or two coats with a roller or brush. The paint should be applied to cool, shaded surfaces—not those in the sun, because heat dries the paint so quickly that it will not adhere properly. Let the paint dry for a week before filling the pool.

Repainting Over Worn-Out Rubber-Base Paint

If the old paint is blistering, peeling or chalking badly throughout the pool, there is nothing for it but to remove it completely right down to the concrete. I have on occasion tried part-way measures with a scraper and electric sander; but even though the remaining paint seemed smooth and tight, moisture invariably got in behind the new paint film and caused an even worse case of blistering than the one I had eradicated.

The easiest, and if you want to be practical about it, the only way to strip all paint from a pool is to have it sandblasted. But this costs $500–$1,000 if you have it done professionally. You may, therefore, want to rent sandblasting equipment from a rental agency and do the work yourself; or you may take the paint off with paint remover.

Following removal of the paint, repair breaks and pits in the concrete with latex cement. Then wash the pool with muriatic acid to etch the concrete and assure good adhesion of the new paint. Rinse well. Roll or brush on two coats of chlorinated rubber or epoxy paint. If the former is used, the concrete must first be allowed to dry for a week or so. Epoxy paint, however, can be applied to concrete which has dried out only a day or two.

Repainting Over Old Epoxy Paint

Epoxy paint can be touched up when it is chipped or scratched, but it should not be completely refinished until it has chalked down for several years to the point where you can almost see the concrete underneath. It must then be thoroughly scraped and sanded to remove loose paint and roughness; or if it is in very poor condition, it should be taken off entirely. Then wash the pool with bleach or trisodium phosphate to get rid of dirt and algae; rinse; wash again with muriatic acid; and rinse once more.

Then apply the primer made for epoxy swimming-pool paint and follow with a single coat of the paint. Observe the manufacturer's directions carefully. Epoxy paint can be applied to slightly damp surfaces, and usually needs to be allowed to dry for only a few days before you start refilling the pool.

Note that rubber-base paints should never be applied over epoxy paint.

173

Repainting Over Old Cement Paint

Cement paint needs to be renewed more often than other pool finishes; but the job is considerably easier. Simply scrape and sand the pool walls and floor to remove loose and powdery paint. Wash with a bleach or trisodium phosphate, and rinse. The new cement paint can then be applied as soon as most of the dampness has disappeared. (There is no need to wait a week or so for a pool which has been full of water to dry.) One coat is enough. Use a rather stiff brush and work the paint well into the surface. After it has dried a couple of days, fill the pool.

If you switch from cement paint to a chlorinated rubber or epoxy, the old paint must be removed by sandblasting and the concrete etched with muriatic acid. After rinsing and drying, apply two coats of the new paint.

Painting a Plastered Pool

Chip out loose plaster and fill all voids with latex cement. Wash the walls and floor with bleach or trisodium phosphate, and rinse. Then repeat the process with muriatic acid. Finish the job with two coats of chlorinated rubber or epoxy paint.

Repainting a Steel Pool

In the early days of the swimming-pool boom a few pools were built out of heavy sheets of steel welded together and then painted. Such construction is almost unknown today; but you may own one of the old pools. These should be emptied annually and examined. Repainting is usually necessary to assure that rust does not start to eat out the metal.

If the old finish is reasonably sound, wash the walls and floor with bleach or trisodium phosphate, and rinse well. Then remove all signs of rust with a scraper, sandpaper or rust remover. Prime the bare metal immediately with a metal conditioner containing phosphoric acid and follow with a coat of rust-inhibiting primer. When this is dry, repaint the entire pool with a paint which is compatible with the old finish.

If the old finish has deteriorated extensively, remove whatever is left by sandblasting. Then, after cleaning off all rust, coat with a metal conditioner, metal primer and finish paint.

Repainting Pool Equipment

Submerged metal must be cleaned thoroughly to remove rust, scale and dirt. Prime bare metal with a rust-inhibiting primer. Then apply epoxy pool paint.

Metal surfaces above ground should be cleaned and primed in the same way. Then apply one or two coats of an oil-based metal enamel made for exterior use.

Repainting a Wooden Diving Board

Wash the board with bleach or trisodium phosphate, and rinse. Fill cracks with plastic wood. Sand carefully, taking pains to remove splinters. Then apply one or two coats of epoxy diving-board paint with an abrasive added to make it skidproof.

Skidproofing Slippery Surfaces Around the Pool

Clean the surfaces and apply epoxy diving-board paint. It adheres as well to concrete, masonry and metal as to wood; is as durable below water as above.

Ordinary epoxy and chlorinated rubber pool paints can also be made skidproof simply by mixing a small quantity of clean, washed, fine building sand into them. Do not use sea sand, which contains salt.

18 Managing the Pool During the Swimming Season

There is much more to running a pool than just keeping it operating and in good operating condition. This is especially true if you allow people outside the family to use it. You must also maintain and enforce good sanitation and safety practices in and around the pool at all times.

This obviously has considerable bearing on who is allowed to use the pool and who is not. But I am not about to recommend here the system you should follow in making your pool available to relatives, friends and neighbors, because that is a very personal matter you alone can settle. Enough to say that such a system is imperative if you are not to be driven out of your own pool by people who contributed nothing to its construction or maintenance and if you don't want to run the risk of lawsuits.

But the rules for using and managing your pool are something else again, because personal preference should not enter in. These are time-tested rules which apply as much to your pool as to mine. In fact, I am not stretching a point to say they apply as much to residential pools as to public pools.

Safety Rules for Swimmers

(1) Never swim alone.

(2) Nonswimmers must not use the pool in the absence from the pool area of a responsible adult or teen-ager who can swim.

(3) Don't swim immediately after meals, when you have been drinking alcohol or when you are overly tired.

(4) Don't swim during thunderstorms.

(5) Don't swim when the water is so murky you cannot see the bottom of the pool.

(6) Horseplaying and rough-housing in and around the pool are prohibited.

(7) Diving is permitted only from the end of the diving board.

(8) Don't use the pool at night unless it is illuminated by an underwater light or high-level lighting around the deck.

(9) Electrical appliances, radios, TV sets, hair dryers, etc., are not permitted within the pool area if electrical circuits are not protected by ground-fault circuit interrupters as described in Chapter 11.

(10) Glass and china articles must not be brought into the pool area and definitely must never be used, carried, etc., on the pool deck.

(11) Learn how to administer artificial respiration.

Sanitation Rules for Swimmers

The following regulations are taken verbatim from a circular of the Illinois Department of Public Health. Designed for public pools, they may seem a little extreme for residential pools. But it's impossible to deny that they make very good sense:

1. Admission to the pool is refused to all persons having any venereal disease, contagious disease, infectious condition such as colds, ringworm, fevers, foot infections, skin lesions, carbuncles, pimples, inflamed eyes, ear discharges, etc., or any other condition which has the appearance of being infectious. Persons with excessive sunburn, abrasion which has not healed, corn plasters, bunion pads, adhesive tape, rubber bandages, etc., or other bandage of any kind will not be admitted.

2. No food, drink, gum, or tobacco will be allowed in the pool area.

3. All persons will be required to take a shower in the nude with soap and warm water before being allowed in the pool area.

4. Bathers who leave the pool area for any reason are required to shower before returning to the pool.

5. All swimmers with long hair are required to wear caps while in the pool.

6. All persons shall report to the instructor or attendant after taking their shower, before entering the water, and shall be subject to any other rules and regulations which the pool management may deem necessary for the good and safety of all.

Sanitation and Safety Rules for the Pool Owner

To prevent the spread of athlete's foot, regularly clean the poolhouse floor, pool deck, diving board (especially if it is covered with a fiber mat) and above-water ladders with a phenol disinfectant, chlorine bleach or solution of calcium hypochlorite. The latter is made by dissolving 5 tsp. of hypochlorite in 1 gal. of warm water. This should be mixed and stored in a plastic, glass or crockery container—not metal. (The fungicidal foot baths which were once fixtures of public pools are no longer considered to be effective against athlete's foot and other foot infections.)

Keep a covered metal garbage can in the pool area for daily collection of food scraps, pop bottles, cigaret butts, etc., which accumulate in the area. And don't forget to add the contents of the can to your regular weekly garbage collections.

Clean out cupboards, drawers, chests, etc., in the poolhouse to discourage mice which may frequent them; and put out traps for the creatures. Mice not only are dirty, but I find that they have a strange facility for drowning themselves in pools and making little girls and big girls scream.

To improve safety on the pool deck and other paved areas (which are said to account for about 80 per cent of all accidents in the pool area), keep them in good repair at all times and don't tolerate slippery areas for a minute. Cracks and holes in a deck can be quickly filled with Portland cement (if the cracks are large) or latex cement. If the deck sinks in one or two spots, try raising it with a crowbar and shoveling gravel underneath. If this doesn't work, bring the sunken areas up to the proper level with a coat of latex cement, which can be troweled to a feather edge. To eliminate slippery spots, scrub the paving with a strong household cleansing powder. Another possibility is to paint the deck with pool paint containing fine sand.

Protecting Yourself Against Lawsuits

Because of differences in the law between states, your legal responsibilities as a pool owner are not completely clear; so you may wish to consult your lawyer before building a pool. But even this may not answer all questions because of frequent changes in the courts' interpretations of our laws. Your best defense against lawsuits, therefore, is to take the following steps:

(1) Make sure you carry sufficient liability insurance either in the form of a straight liability policy or a homeowner's policy.

(2) Observe all state and local ordinances regarding the construction and management of pools and the fencing of pool areas.

(3) In a conspicuous place near the pool, post a set of clearly typed rules which spell out (a) the conditions under which the pool and pool area may be used; (b) standards of conduct for pool users, and (c) any dangerous conditions which may exist in the pool area such as a slippery deck surface or tricky diving board.

(4) When an adult member of your family is in attendance at the pool and in effect supervising it, see that he enforces the posted rules for using the pool.

(5) If you live in a state in which a swimming pool has been ruled to constitute an attractive nuisance (meaning that it is an attraction to children who are too young to appreciate the peril), make doubly certain to bar all access to the pool when it is not in use. As further protection, you might screen the pool from public

178

view and forbid all children who cannot swim from entering the pool area at any time. (The theory here is that if a child cannot see a pool or is not allowed to use it, he is less likely to be attracted to it.)

(6) Inspect the pool and all pool equipment frequently and keep them in safe-to-use condition.

(7) If your pool is built to the National Swimming Pool Institute's minimum standards (Chapter 3), make certain that any new or replacement diving board you install is sized specifically to the pool.

19 Cleaning the Pool

It is a sad fact that you no sooner start filling a new swimming pool than you must go out and buy tools to keep it clean. Actually, I suppose this comes as no more of a shock than the realization that you must buy chemicals to keep the water pure. But whereas the purification of water has a certain amount of fascination, cleaning the pool is, well, just another cleaning chore.

I can suggest no way to make it more palatable. No inexpensive way, that is. Recent years have brought some remarkable equipment for automatically cleaning pools while you sleep, and statistics indicate that this is catching on nicely. But the price of the equipment gives me, at least, pause. I think I'll muddle along cleaning my pool by hand for a while longer. After all, it isn't a mean or nasty chore; and even at its worst, I doubt that it takes more than an hour a week.

Cleaning the Pool Plumbing

For how to clean your filter, see Chapter 17. As a rule, cleaning is necessary about once a week.

The strainer in the skimmer should be lifted out and cleaned daily. That in the pump generally need not be checked except when you clean the filter; but if you don't have a modern skimmer, much more frequent cleaning is called for.

Surface Cleaning

Removing hair, leaves, grass clippings, insects, dirt and even an occasional dead mouse, mole or bird from the surface of the pool is almost a daily task; but if the skimmer in the pool wall is working properly, there isn't very much to do. I never cease to be amazed at the amount of debris which collects in and must be removed from the skimmer strainer basket every 24 hours. Yet in spite of this, it is usually necessary to walk around the pool with a hand skimmer—known usually as a leaf skimmer—and scoop out the particles which are left (mainly on the pool walls at the scum line).

Hand skimmers are made of fine plastic mesh held in a semi-rigid steel or plastic frame on the end of a long aluminum handle. They are such a simple tool that the normal temptation is to buy the cheapest available; but after breaking three or four of these, I discovered the error of my ways.

The best skimmer (costing about $8, not counting the handle) has a more or less square, metal (therefore unbreakable) frame roughly 15 in. across with enough mesh to form a basket about 4 in. deep. The square is preferable to the more common curved design because it scoops debris from the surface more efficiently; and it is far and away better for picking leaves and twigs off the bottom of a pool.

An 8-ft. handle on the skimmer is long enough for most pools, because even though you may not be able to reach to the center of a large pool, the basket stirs up enough current to send debris scooting across the surface to the sides. However, it's a good idea to use a handle which can be extended to 16 or 20 ft. so you can remove large debris from the bottom at the deep end of the pool.

A useful supplement to a leaf skimmer is a so-called leaf rake made specifically for cleaning the pool bottom. It is simply an extra-wide, extra-deep rectangular skimmer. The dimensions of a rake retailing at $13 (without handle) are 22 in. wide, 6 in. from front to back and 8 in. deep.

Brushes for Bottom Cleaning

Several tools are needed to clean the walls and floor of a pool; and since all require long handles, one of the first (minor) decisions you must make is whether each tool should have its own permanent handle or whether you should buy a single handle with an end adapter which permits changing quickly from one tool to another. My not-very-firm choice is for individual permanent handles simply because they save a little time and exasperation in the cleaning operation. But lower cost and easier storage are good arguments in favor of the interchangeable handle.

Actually, except for the adapter head, there is no difference between permanent and interchangeable handles. They are made of aluminum tubing about 1¼ in. in diameter. One type of handle has a telescoping arrangement which allows you to convert an 8-ft. tube into a 16-ft. tube simply by pulling out the inner tube and locking it in place with a plastic ferrule. (There are also 12-ft. tubes which extend to 24 ft.; and 16's which extend to 32 ft.) The other type of handle is made in 6- or 12-ft. sections which are joined together with built-in clips much like the wands on a household vacuum cleaner.

The basic cleaning tool which is used at the end of a handle is a slender 18-in.-wide nylon bristle brush. The most popular design is slightly curved at the ends so it can be used to clean rounded as well as flat surfaces. All pool owners need the brush to remove loose sediment from the walls daily. In addition, some people use

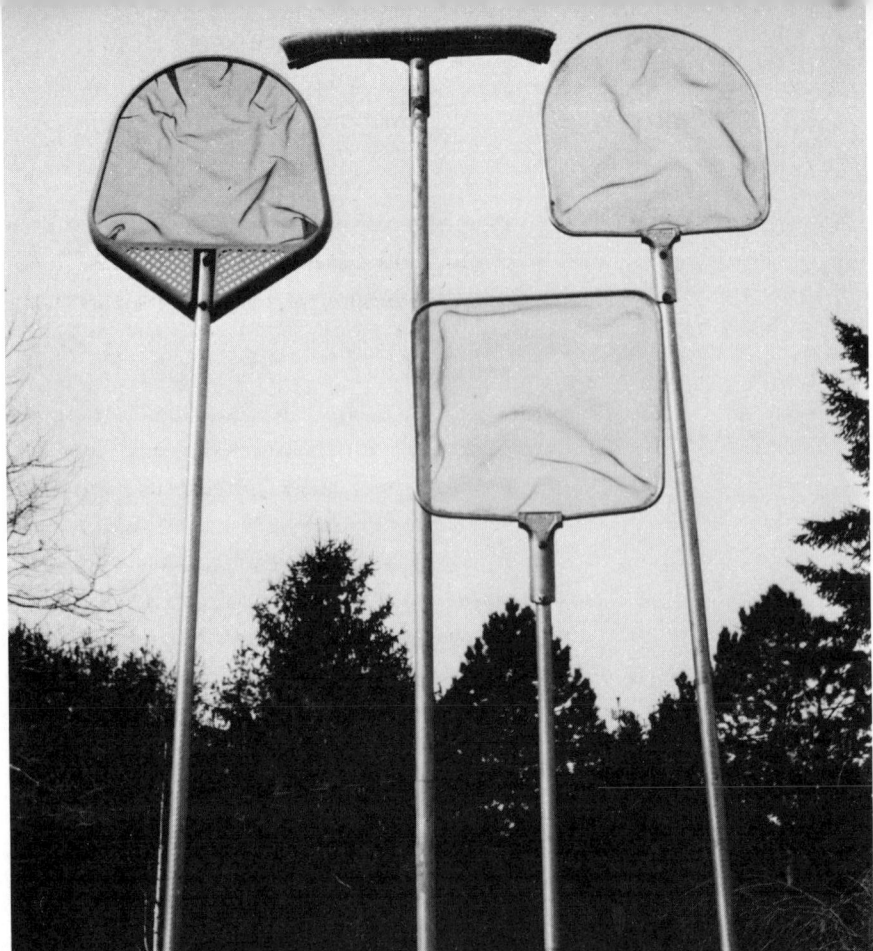

An 18-inch-wide pool brush surrounded by three types of hand skimmer. The skimmer at left has a breakable plastic frame but its unusually deep net makes it very efficient. The two skimmers at right have strong steel frames, somewhat shallower nets.

the brush to thorough-clean their pools by pushing the dirt on the bottom to the main drain. However, since this roils the water considerably and may overload the filter, it is a good practice only in very small pools and/or in pools in which the dirt consists primarily of rather big, heavy particles which do not make the water turbid as they are pushed toward the drain.

Other cleaning tools which you may need—although you don't have to invest in them until the need has been established—are a small brush with nylon or fiber bristles, another small brush with stainless-steel bristles, a pumice block and a magnet. The nylon-fiber brush is used for acid-washing and scrubbing stained and scummy ceramic tiles at the water line and removing mild stains on all other surfaces. The stainless-steel brush is for tough stains, encrusted dirt and scale deposits on plaster and concrete. The block of pumice, a very fine abrasive, is also used for difficult stains and encrustations on tile and concrete. (Neither of the latter tools should be used on fiberglass or vinyl.) The magnet is used to pick up hairpins and other steel objects from the bottom of the pool before they rust and make stains.

Manual Vacuum Cleaning   A vacuum cleaner is essential if you have a vinyl-liner pool without a main drain; and it is advisable bordering on the essential in all other pools because it removes dirt from the bottom without stirring it up and placing it in suspension.

A manual vacuum is an assemblage of three parts: a long aluminum handle identical with those described above, a flexible hose and a cleaning head.

The hose is made of an accordion-pleated plastic which floats even when full of water. The standard diameter for residential vacuums is 1½ in. Lengths range from 25 to 50 ft., but unless you have an unusually large pool, the shortest length is adequate. With increased length, the suction tends to decline.

The cleaning head which picks up dirt and funnels it into the hose is usually supported on a fringe of stiff bristles, but some heads also have casters. Heads for concrete pools may be made of alu-

Four types of manual vacuum cleaner head. The one at top right is made of flexible plastic so it will bend toward the handle and thus conform to rounded pool bottoms.

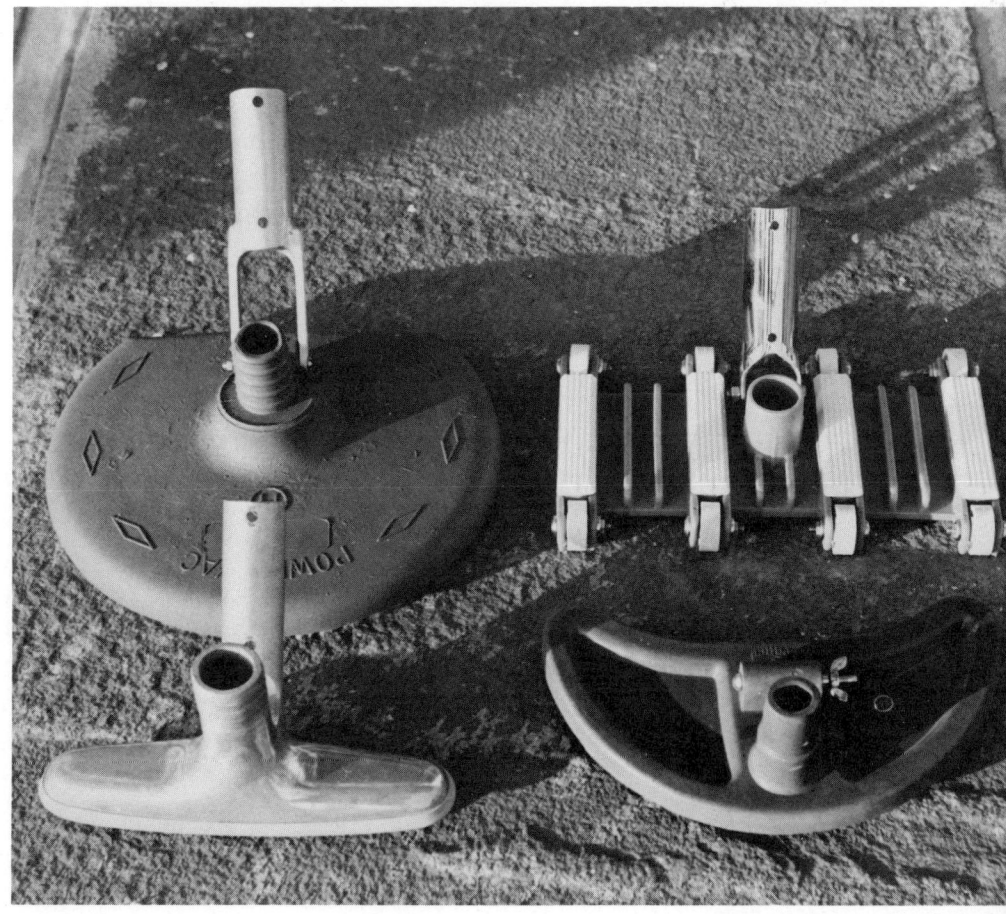

minum or heavy molded rubber; but for a vinyl-liner pool only a rubber head should be used. Head selection also depends on the contours of the pool. If your pool has flat surfaces and sharp corners, a slender rectangular or triangular head should be used. In a pool with irregular surfaces and rounded corners, use a round or bow-shaped head. One unusual head is a rectangular unit mounted on eight casters and made of flexible plastic so it will conform to all contours.

How often you vacuum your pool depends on the dirt load, on the normal suction through the main drain, and on how much you use your 18-in. brush to move dirt to the main drain. In the average pool, once-a-week vacuuming is usually enough.

To use a vacuum, attach the handle and the hose to the head and lower the assemblage to the bottom of the pool. Before attaching the other end of the hose to the vacuum outlet in the pool wall or to the skimmer (if that serves as the vacuum outlet), hold it against the water inlet and fill it with water. This drives the air out of the hose so that when it is attached to the vacuum outlet, air will not enter the suction line and stop the pump.

If there is a separate pipe line from the vacuum outlet to the pump, open the valve controlling the line. To increase the suction at the vacuum head, close or partially close the valves on the main drain line and skimmer line.

If the filter has been recently cleaned and there is not a great deal of dirt in the pool, you can leave the multiport valve on the filter in normal filtering position. Thus the dirt is drawn into the filter for later removal by backwashing. It is better practice, however, to set the multiport valve at "drain" so that the dirt and water taken in through the vacuum bypasses the filter and is discharged to waste. You should never use the vacuum when the filter is set at "backwash" because large particles picked up from the bottom might clog the filter.

In the case of DE filters which have a regeneration cycle and cartridge filters, water from the pool simply pours into the tank, leaves its load of dirt and returns to the pool. The filters are then cleaned in the usual manner described in Chapter 8.

In contrast with a household vacuum cleaner, a pool vacuum does not have to be moved in any set pattern to clean effectively. Work in long strokes or short strokes; across the pool or lengthwise—it doesn't matter. The main aims are to cover all areas, to stir up as little sediment as possible and to work fast so that you don't waste any more water than necessary.

Jet Vacuums   Jet vacuums differ from conventional pool vacuums in that they are hitched up, not to the pump and filter, but to a garden hose which brings in water from the house plumbing system. Through a Venturi effect, the pressure of the incoming water creates in the cleaning head a suction which picks up dirt from the pool bottom and deposits it in a bag attached to the top of the cleaning head. The main advantage of this system is that the dirt is not collected in the pool filter and there is no loss of pool water. A secondary advantage is that you can pick up leaves and twigs quickly and in large volume without running the risk of clogging the pool plumbing system or without resorting to awkward, very-long-handled leaf skimmers.

On the other side of the coin, jet vacuums are efficient only if the pressure of the incoming water is 50 lb. or over. This exceeds the water pressure available in many homes. Furthermore, to maintain such pressure at the cleaning head, you should use a ¾-in.-diameter hose not more than 50 ft. in length.

Another problem with jet vacuums is that very fine sediment escapes through the bags back into the pool.

This jet vacuum with unusually large bag is designed primarily for collecting leaves on the pool bottom. Turned upside down, it can also be used to skim leaves and debris from the surface of the water. (PHOTO BY JANDY PRODUCTS)

In this automatic cleaner, which moves around the surface of a pool, water from the filter enters through the buoy-supported tube and comes out under pressure through two underwater hoses. The gyrations of the hoses coupled with the jets of water they emit drive dirt to the main drain. Water also jets from the top and side of the cleaner head to wash down the upper walls of the pool. (PHOTO BY ARNESON PRODUCTS, INC.)

Automatic Cleaning

Two basic types of automatic cleaner are now in use in swimming pools. One is suggestive of an upright household vacuum cleaner. It consists of a rather large, motor-driven, wheel-mounted base with a suction inlet. Mounted above this is a canister with a cartridge filter which removes the dirt from the incoming water and returns the filtered water to the pool. Electric power is brought to the unit by a heavy-duty cord plugged into a grounded outlet on the pool deck.

In operation the vacuum cleaner automatically rolls up and down and across the pool, pulling in dirt as it goes. It will clean a small pool in about an hour. Since it operates independently of the pool plumbing system, it does not overload the filter with dirt. On the other hand, if the cleaner itself becomes clogged with dirt, you must stop it and clean it out before continuing with the vacuuming. In addition, the cleaner may have difficulty negotiating very steep inclines; and for this reason, you must brush down the pool walls so that it can pick up the sediment which accumulates there.

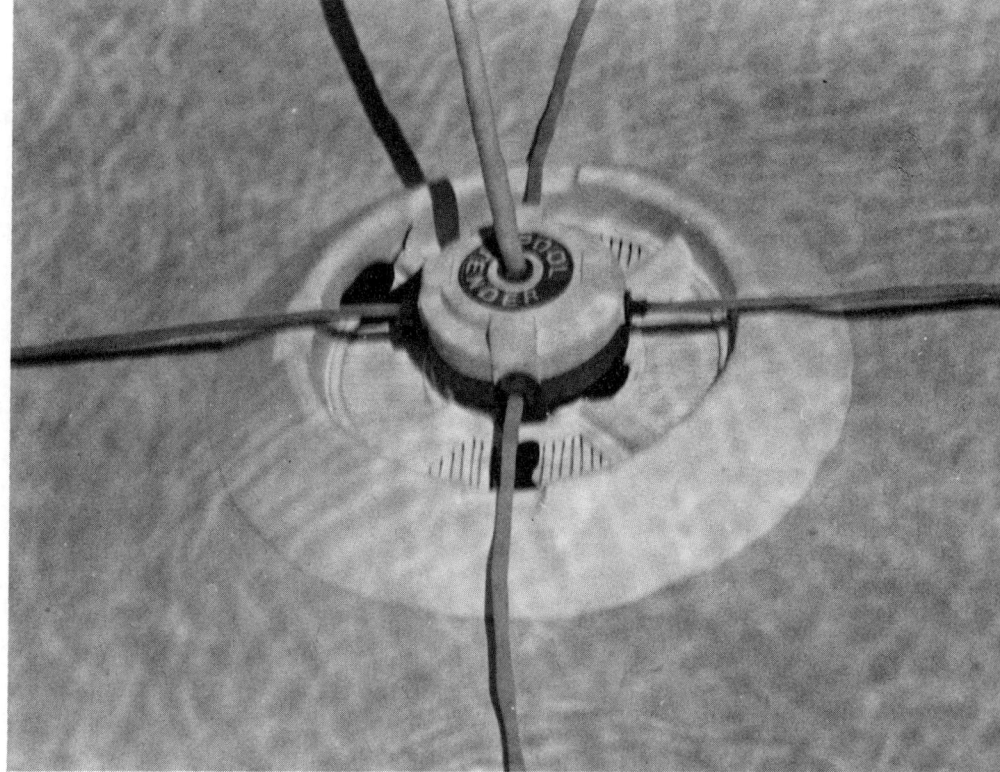

Placed on the bottom of a pool, this automatic cleaner drives dirt toward the main drain with water jets from the four slender, horizontal hoses. When one part of the pool is clean, the cleaner is moved to another part. (PHOTO BY PARAMOUNT LEISURE INDUSTRIES)

The second type of automatic cleaner is suggestive of an octopus. It is not a vacuum. On the contrary, dirt is removed from the pool walls and floor by forcing water from the filter through long, flexible hoses which whip back and forth inside the pool and spit out jets of water that direct the dirt to the main drain and skimmer, from whence it is sucked back into the pool filter.

Most cleaners of this type have a central head to which the hoses are attached. In one unit which retails for $80, the head is placed on the bottom of the pool; and after the hoses have swept the dirt from the surrounding 24-ft.-diameter area, the head is lifted and moved to another part of the pool to complete the job. In a second, more elaborate cleaner costing over $500, the head travels around the pool on the water surface. The unit may be controlled by an automatic time clock.

In another version of the octopus cleaner, the hoses are built into the walls of the pool at the time the pool is constructed. When the system is turned on, the hoses extend out into the pool. At the end of the cleaning period, they retract into the wall.

187

Chemicals for Special Cleaning Operations

Special cleaning agents are necessary only for removing difficult stains and scale deposits. Muriatic acid is the old standby, although it must be used sparingly on concrete and plaster to avoid serious etching of the finish. Trisodium phosphate and strong household detergents used for general-purpose cleaning are safer and may be equally effective on stains, though not on scale. Special detergents sold in swimming-pool stores usually under the name of "ceramic tile and vinyl cleaner" are also good.

My favorite cleaner, however, is nothing more than undiluted chlorine. Although for some reason there is little support for this choice in swimming-pool literature, I have found chlorine more effective on more types of pool stains than anything else. And the nice thing about it is that it does not introduce to the pool any new chemicals which work in opposition to your carefully balanced water.

Use chlorine bleach on stains above water or in an empty pool; use chlorine powder below water. Simply sprinkle it heavily on a stain or wrap a handful in a soft cloth and scrub the stain.

Note: Never use steel wool for cleaning pools, because it disintegrates in chlorinated water. Use bronze wool or a copper or stainless steel scouring pad, or simply a stiff fiber brush or nubby nylon scouring pad.

Cleaning the Pool Deck and Surrounding Area

Daily cleaning of the deck and every-other-day cleaning of the adjacent area is essential to sanitation and safety and to keeping the pool as free as possible of the dirt and debris that may be blown in, washed in or carried in on swimmers' feet. The ideal machine for the purpose is a gasoline-driven outdoor vacuum cleaner which will suck up all but the heaviest debris from rough as well as smooth surfaces. It costs about $175, but can be used anywhere on your property and usually can be converted in the autumn to a leaf blower.

The alternative is to use an electric shop vacuum cleaner or an ordinary broom and dustpan. They save a great deal of money but are effective only on paved surfaces. For this reason, if you have grass surrounding the pool deck, you should be sure to equip the mower with a grass-catcher.

For other deck-cleaning operations, see Chapter 18.

20 Troubleshooting Pool Problems

Many of the problems encountered in swimming-pool operation are readily soluble by the pool owner. Others are not. But before you call for help—which may be slow in arriving and which may not be as knowledgeable as it should be—it always pays to try to pin down what is wrong and then see if you can't correct matters yourself.

The following are relatively common problems:

Water Level Dropping Abnormally If you live in a very hot, dry climate, this may be the result of evaporation, in which case the only possible solution is to cover the pool during the day when not in use. The alternative is to pour on the water a liquid which forms a thin, invisible monomolecular film. This is used not only to reduce evaporation from outdoor pools and escape of water vapor from indoor pools but also to prevent loss of heat from heated pools. Use 1 or 2 oz., depending on brand, for each 125 sq. ft. of water surface. Make repeat applications every two or three days.

A more likely cause of water loss is an active leak. If this occurs in the walls or floor of a concrete pool, the best repair is made by drawing the water down below the leak. To seal a crack, cut it open to a depth of about ¾ in. with a cold chisel and blow out all the crumbs. Then fill it tight with hydraulic cement, and let it set for at least 12 hours before painting and refilling the pool. Latex, vinyl or epoxy cements may also be used if the crack is first dried out with a heat lamp.

If the leak is through a joint in a concrete pool or in the fiberglass walls of a pool, clean out the old sealing compound as well as possible. Dry the surfaces thoroughly. And fill with polysulfide rubber sealant. Silicone rubber sealant (usually sold as bathtub caulking) is also excellent; but since many brands will not hold paint, you should use the white sealant only in white pools.

If it is impractical to lower the water to fix a crack or open joint, use an epoxy putty designed for underwater repairs.

Holes in vinyl liners are repaired with vinyl patching material. Some patches are stuck down with special cement sold with the patches; others come with a pressure-sensitive adhesive on one side. In either case, the patches can be used under water as well as above.

Leaks in pipe lines are easy to locate above ground but are almost impossible to find below ground unless they are so active that they make the ground soggy or unless they can be detected with a stethoscopelike device used by water utilities. Be that as it may, once you have pinpointed a leak, the only reliable way to control it is to cut out that section of pipe and replace with new. However, so-called temporary repairs which often prove to be surprisingly permanent are easily made with clamps. If the pipe is copper or steel, turn off the pump and clean the area around the hole thoroughly with steel wool. Then cut rubber gasket material or an old tire tube to fit over the hole and tighten this down with steel mending clamps made specifically for repairing pipes or the stainless-steel clamps used in joining plastic pipe (shown in the illustration on page 63). If plastic pipe is leaking, turn off the pump and dry the area around the leak. Then squeeze silicone rubber sealant into and over the hole. Let this set; then apply stainless-steel clamps.

To repair a leak at a joint in a copper pipe, clean the joint with steel wool until the metal and solder are bright. Then heat with a propane torch until a new strip of solder applied to the joint melts and is drawn into the joint by capillarity.

In a steel pipe, the joint must be completely taken apart and cleaned. Then smear pastelike pipe dope into the threads or wrap pipe tape around them, and screw the pieces back together again.

In plastic pipe, simply tightening the stainless-steel clamps may stop leaks at joints. If not, loosen the clamps and pull the joint apart. Smear silicone rubber sealant into the threads of the fitting, force them into the pipe and retighten the clamps.

Leaks in the pump or filter may occur simply because drain plugs are not tight. But for such problems as a defective seal in the pump or a multiport valve which leaks water to the drain line when set at "filter," you need expert help.

Pump Running Too Slow or Too Hot

The impeller or shaft may not be turning freely, in which case you should call in a serviceman. Or the voltage at the pump may be low. To check this you need an electrical contractor. Overheating of the motor may also be because it's installed in a cramped place which does not afford adequate ventilation.

Note that if you can hold your hand for a minute or two on a motor while it is running, it is not overheated. Pump motors are generally designed to run 72° above the air temperature. This means that on a 70° day, the motor can be expected to run at as much as 142°—a temperature higher than the hand can stand for any length of time.

Pump Suddenly Runs Very Slow or Stops

If you have had no previous trouble with the pump and if other appliances and motors on your property are also acting strangely, the problem is a voltage drop on the power lines. To protect the pump motor, turn it off at the switch and do not restart it until full power is restored. (All other large motors should also be shut off.)

Pump Not Pumping

Make sure it is primed and that all valves are open. If you have replaced an old filter system with a new system, it is possible that the old piping is no longer properly sized to the pump; and the pump therefore does not pull in water. This can be corrected by closing or opening the valves on the suction and return lines until pumping starts.

A more serious problem is caused by air leaks in the suction line. For instance, if the water level in a pool falls so low that air is drawn into the skimmer even for only a second or two, a pump may lose its prime and stop pumping. This particular difficulty can be corrected by adding water to the pool. Many air leaks, however, are much less obvious.

The first place to check for them is at the joints in the suction line. If trouble still continues, your only recourse is to call in the pool builder or a serviceman to check the entire system.

Pump Not Pumping Enough Water

The motor and pump may be running too slow because of low voltage. Valves in the suction and return lines may be partially closed. The strainer in the pump and/or skimmer may be clogged. The filter may be dirty. All these problems, except the first, are easily corrected.

If the problem continues, it may be that some object has plugged the suction line. (I once found my system clogged by an immature peach which had fallen out of the tree near my pool and which had somehow been sucked through the grating over the main drain and through the pipe right up to the opening into the pump.) To correct this, open the valves in the line wide and see if the object is drawn into the strainer. If not, try pushing a stiff wire from the pump into the suction line to break up the object (if you are lucky enough to hit it) or pull it out. If this fails, hold one end of the vacuum-cleaner hose over the inlet on the return line and push the other end of the hose down into the skimmer. The force of the water from the return may loosen the stoppage in the suction line. If the stoppage persists, open the line at a joint and run a plumber's snake through it.

Pump Noisy
This may be caused by bad bearings or misalignment of the impeller; if so, you need professional help. But the trouble may also be cavitation, a common problem characterized by rumbling or growling sounds in the pump, by erratic pressure gauges, by air bubbles in the water discharged from the pump and eventually by diminished flow. All this results from the fact that the pump is starved for water.

The cure is simple and should be attempted immediately, because continuation of cavitation will destroy the pump. Simply throttle down the valve in the *return* line until the noise stops; and leave the valve at this setting.

Filtering Action Inadequate
This may result from the fact that the pool is excessively dirty or it may be that the filter needs normal cleaning. If after cleaning a sand filter you find that the problem continues and that there is a greater difference than usual between the pressure-gauge readings, it is probably because filter action has been restricted by excessive dirt, debris or scale accumulation. To correct this, use a prepared filter-cleaning compound according to the maker's directions.

If the filtering action of a DE filter is inadequate after normal cleaning, clean the filter with a special cleaning compound or remove the filter elements and soak and gently scrub them in warm detergent solution or dilute muriatic acid.

Poor filter action in a cartridge filter usually indicates the need for replacing the cartridges.

Pool Heater Doesn't Fire Up
Be sure the pilot light is on. If it is and the heater still doesn't start, clean the strainer in the skimmer and pump and clean the filter thoroughly. This should do the trick. If not, call a serviceman.

192

Wet-Niche Light Burns Out

Shut off the power at the fuse box or circuit breaker. Remove the light from its niche by lying on your stomach on the deck, reaching down and pulling it out, or by getting into the pool. The light has a long cord which should come out with it; but if this sticks, pour liquid detergent down into the deck junction box.

Bring the light up on the deck and before taking it apart note carefully the manner in which the housing, lens and front chrome ring are assembled. Then disassemble the light and make sure all parts are in good condition. Clean the lens. Install a new bulb and new lens gasket to assure a tight seal. See that the seal at the point where the cord enters the fixture is water-tight.

Restore power at the fuse box or circuit breaker and turn on the light switch *for just a second* to determine whether the bulb lights. Then turn off all power again and reassemble the fixture. Before replacing it in the pool, put it in a pail of water and turn it on to make certain no bubbles are escaping through an imperfect seal. Turn off the power once again and replace the fixture in the niche in the pool wall. When doing so, coil the excess cord around the light so it won't be crushed.

Remember never to burn a wet-niche light fixture out of water for more than an instant; otherwise the heat will ruin it.

Pool Water Cloudy

Test the water for total alkalinity and pH. If too high, add acid to bring the levels down. Clean the filter.

If you have a DE filter, cloudiness is usually caused by diatomaceous earth returning to the pool. In this case, drain the filter and make sure the filter element has not been damaged; then precoat it again.

Pool Water Reddish-Brown

This is usually caused by iron precipitated out of the water by chlorine. Add an iron-control chemical to the pool.

Pool Water Green

Water may start out green if it contains iron and then turn reddish-brown. But if you have a green color which persists, the cause is probably either copper in the water or algae. To correct these problems, bring the pH to the proper level. Then add calcium hypochlorite at the rate of 1 oz. per 500 gal. and run the filter until the color disappears. Then clean the filter.

The alternative, if algae are present, is to treat the pool with an

193

algicide. But if algae have developed too far to respond to these treatments, the only thing you can do is to drain the pool and scrub it thoroughly with dilute muriatic acid.

Pool Water Brownish-Black
Manganese is the troublemaker. Treat the water as for a green coloration.

Pool Water Has an Unpleasant Odor
Shock-treat the pool with 1 oz. of calcium hypochlorite per 500 gal. of water.

Pool Water Irritating to the Eyes
Test for pH: it may be too high or too low. There may also be excess chlorine in the water; but if so, it will dissipate fairly quickly.

Pool Ladder and Other Metal Objects in the Pool Corroding
The pH is probably below 7.0. Increase it by adding soda ash. Remember, however, that ordinary iron and steel, and even galvanized steel once the coating is broken, will rust in any water. Cheap chrome-plated fittings will also corrode.

Pool Overflows Because of a Heavy Storm
Let it. No serious harm will be done unless the overflow floods an adjacent building. After the storm, pump the pool down to normal level. See next problem.

A Hurricane Is on the Way
Don't bother pumping down the pool until after the storm (see above). But turn off all power to the pool area, and store furniture and other loose items in a building. If the pump is in an exposed location, remove the motor or wrap it well in plastic to keep out driving water and sand. After the storm, super-chlorinate the pool and take out all large debris before starting the pump.

21 Putting the Pool to Bed for the Winter*

The more carefully you winterize your pool, the earlier you can use it the following spring. Furthermore, you may save money on unnecessary repairs.

How you go about the job depends primarily on whether you cover the pool. If you do, the first step in winterizing it is to get the water crystal clear. True, it will not stay that way through the winter. But the cleaner the water is in the fall, the cleaner it will be next spring.

To clean the water, follow your usual method of treatment; remove debris from the surface; and pull out whatever is on the bottom with your vacuum. Then clean the filter thoroughly.

The next step (which is the first step in winterizing an uncovered pool) is to switch the filter to "drain" and draw down the pool. If you have a solid pool cover, the winter water level should be several inches below the vacuum, skimmer and inlet lines. But if you have a semiporous cover (or no cover at all), the water level should not only be below these lines but should also be far enough below the coping so that the rain and snow entering the pool over the course of the winter will not reach the coping and damage it by freezing. (In other words, if your normal precipitation from, say, November 1 to May 1 totals 18 in., pump out the pool until the water is at least 18 in. below the bottom of the coping.)

At this point the rulebook says that the vacuum, skimmer and inlet lines must be drained to keep them from freezing and breaking. It was several years before I heard this, however, so I never did it—and I never suffered the consequences, because all the piping in my system is made of flexible plastic tubing which resists freezing damage. If you have plastic pipe, you can follow my example or not, as you wish. But if you have metal pipe, draining is a must.

Hopefully, after the pool level is drawn down below the pipe lines, the lines will empty naturally when you open the pump and filter to drain them. But this is not a foregone conclusion; so if you have never gone through the draining process before, you should open the lines themselves at the filter and force air through them with the blower end of a vacuum cleaner. If no water comes out, it may be assumed henceforth that the lines drain themselves.

* Reprinted in part from *Pools & Gardens*, © 1972.

To keep water from getting into the lines during the winter, close them with winterizing plugs available from your pool dealer. Some skimmers must also be protected with special plugs.

Draining the main drain line just below the pump is unnecessary since the water in it drops naturally to the level of the pool. In mild climates, this is likely to be below the frost line. In cold climates, when the water freezes, it will expand upward in the empty line rather than against the pipe walls.

Complete draining of the pump and filter is more important than draining of the pipes; but it is also easier. You simply unscrew the drain plugs at the base of the units and open the units at the top to admit air. You can leave the plugs off all winter; but if there is a possibility of water entering, they should be closed.

If you neglect to drain either the pump or filter before minus-32° temperatures freeze the water in them, you should immediately erect some sort of enclosure around them and set an electric heater inside until the ice melts and can be drained off.

Removal of the pump motor is unnecessary unless it is in a pit which is subject to flooding; however, if you have not been satisfied with its performance, this is a good time to take it to the pool dealer or a motor-repair service for a check-up. If you leave the motor in place, wrap it tightly in plastic to keep out snow. (Even with this protection, however, you should make a practice of shoveling deep snow away from the motor so there is no chance of its becoming water-soaked.)

On the other hand, you should remove the pressure gauges on the filter because they are often damaged by winter weather.

The pool heater must also be drained completely and for best results you should have it blown out with air. Leave the drain open. Remove the pressure relief valve.

Remove the automatic chlorinator and store it in a dry place after cleaning.

In cold climates, to keep ice from breaking underwater lights, pull the fuse, remove the lights from their niches and lower them gently into the water. If the wires are too short to permit resting the lights on the bottom of the pool, the lights must be suspended by ropes from the deck.

In mild climates, where the pool water does not freeze deep enough to damage lights, they can be left in their niches.

Most pool accessories should also be removed from in and around the pool. These include the rope around the sides, ther-

How one pool owner puts his pool to bed for the winter: the wet-niche underwater light is stored on the deck; the diving board has been removed from its modern pedestal and stored under cover with the slide, which is normally installed in the four deck anchors.

mometer, ladder, handrails, diving board and slide. Actually, some of these things, such as the slide and a modern diving board, are quite unharmed by weather but must be removed simply because they get in the way of the pool cover. But the ladder is another matter. I foolishly left mine in the pool one winter and the ice pushed it up and away from the wall so badly that the deck cracked at the point where the ladder was attached.

Store all accessories under cover if possible. Be careful not to place anything heavy on top of the diving board lest you warp it.

The next step in the closing-down operation is to treat the

197

water to discourage algae. All pool dealers have special chemical kits for this purpose; but you can do just as well with a heavy dose of chlorine. Use about 1 oz. of calcium hypochlorite for each 500 gal. of water. (This treatment is omitted if you don't have a pool cover because the chlorine will be dissipated rapidly.)

Now pull the cover over the pool and weight the edges down securely. If the cover is semiporous, no steps need be taken to keep it from sagging, since water accumulating on it will drip through and slowly raise the level of the pool. But sagging is a problem with a solid cover unless you hump it up above the water with "pillows" or use a pump to remove water collecting on it (see Chapter 9).

The time-honored practice of tying logs or partially weighted plastic jugs around two or three sides of a pool in order to reduce pressure against the walls as the water freezes is no longer widely followed. Most well-built pools are crack-resistant; consequently, the only damage you can predictably expect from ice is to paint and ceramic tile on the upper part of the walls.

On the other hand, if a pool which is not covered is used for ice skating, logs, boards or other forms of protection must be fastened around the pool to keep skaters from damaging the walls and coping.

The final step in winterizing your pool is to clear out the poolhouse. Remove towels, clothing, bathing suits, paper goods, articles that may rust and anything mice may eat. Seal packages of dry pool chemicals and either leave them in the poolhouse or store them in some other cool, dry place out of reach of children. Bring liquid chemicals into the basement where they cannot freeze, but keep them away from the furnace.

If You Live in a Mild Climate

In areas where freezing weather rarely strikes but where it is too cold for swimming, normal summer pool care should be maintained throughout the winter but on a reduced basis. Instead of running the filter for 12–24 hours a day, you can reduce operation to the daylight hours or even less without affecting water clarity. Chemical treatment can also be cut down. If you keep the pH and total alkalinity at the proper levels, a good chlorination schedule is as follows: While the water temperature is between 70° and 60°, add sufficient chlorine every other day to maintain a 0.6–1.0 ppm residual. With the water temperature at 60°–55°, chlorinate twice a week; at 55°–50°, chlorinate once a week; at 50°–45°, chlorinate every two weeks; at 45°–40°, chlorinate once a month. But be prepared to increase dosage sharply at any time when a sudden warm spell occurs.

Covering the pool keeps it free of debris and reduces chlorine loss. But unless the pool is tucked off in a corner where it cannot be seen, the cover will turn one of the most attractive parts of any garden into an eyesore. That's one thing wrong with pool covers: they are not pretty.

22 Above-ground Pools

It is quite clear that this book is not about above-ground pools. Visually, they are an abomination; and if a family owns its own home and values its appearance, the only possible excuses for buying such a pool are the following:

• The property is large enough so the pool can be completely screened from view without detriment to the use and beauty of the remaining land.

• The lot has such a steep slope that the cost of constructing an in-ground pool would be exorbitant. In this situation, the family might build a wood deck out from the hillside, suspend an above-ground pool in this and rest the bottom of the pool on a lower deck.

• The pool is to be used as a test to determine whether the family really wants and will use a pool.

• The pool is for temporary use only—for example, to be used for therapeutic purposes by a person recovering from an accident or illness, or to be used for recreation while plans for an in-ground pool are being completed.

• The family is renting its home.

• The family owns its home but expects to move within a year or so.

Pool Design and Installation

The typical above-ground pool has vertical sidewalls made usually of aluminum but sometimes of wood, and a tough, one-piece vinyl liner which covers the floor and the walls up to the coping. A deck surrounds the pool at the level of the coping. This is reached by a ladder or flight of steps from the ground outside the pool, and is itself surrounded by a fence to keep swimmers from falling to the ground. The pump and filter are installed at ground level under the deck. In many cases, the entire structure is wrapped in a light-weight aluminum skirt which conceals the underpinnings of the deck and the wall supports.

Most above-ground pools are 4 ft. deep and have a flat bottom. To build these, it is necessary only to level the ground, firm it well and cover it with a 2-in. cushion of sand to assure that the liner is smooth and is not penetrated by rocks in the soil. A few large above-ground pools, however, have 6-ft.-deep sloping bottoms at one end; and in these cases, after the ground is leveled for the pool walls and the floor at the shallow end, it is dug out and shaped at the deep end to fit the liner.

In shape and size, the pools vary considerably. The biggest sellers are round pools less than 20 ft. in diameter. But there are also rectangles, octagons, figure-eights and even kidney shapes. The maximum size is approximately 20 by 40 ft.

Filters are of the high-rate sand, DE or cartridge type. In the least expensive pools, water is drawn from the pool by a hose draped over the coping and returned to the pool by another hose. Better pools have skimmer outlets through which water is drawn from the pool. It is then returned through an inlet in one of the pool walls. A vacuum cleaner is used to clean the bottom of the pool. Still other pools have a main drain in the bottom as well as a skimmer and return.

Whatever the design and installation of the pump and filter, it is imperative that the system be grounded.

Operating an Above-ground Pool

The only difference between the operation of an above-ground and in-ground pool is that the former is smaller but is usually used by the same number of people; consequently, the water contains more contaminants per gallon and free chlorine residual is more difficult to maintain. Filtering and chemical treatment must therefore be given extremely careful attention.

The actual duration of filter operation and method of treating the pool are identical with that described in earlier chapters.

Safety and sanitation rules are also the same. However, because the pool is 4 ft. above ground and already surrounded by a wall, construction of a fence around it may not be required. But when the pool is not in use, the ladder to the deck should be removed or pushed up out of a child's reach. During long shut-downs, the pool should also be topped with a sturdy cover which is locked in place.

In winter the pool is covered with a water-tight cover supported by pillows so water will run off to the sides. The pillows also absorb pressure from ice.

INDEX

Index